MY RECOVERY FROM BRAIN CANCER

Gemma Hoefkens

CONTENTS

1. Before cancer
2. The Biopsy
3. Treatment
4. Homoeopathy
5. Bewdley
6. Lemon Drizzle Cake
7. Something Worth Considering
8. Medical notes and research on homoeopathy

PROLOGUE

I just caught myself. I'm just sitting on a train going to a homoeopathy college to do a talk on, well, ME! I can't believe it, I'm so excited, exhilarated even.

I text Janice, Can you believe it? It is 8 yrs since I was told I was going to die now I'm doing a talk about it. Thanx again for all your help. Yr FAB.
Gemma :0) xxx"

So, of course I'm eager to tell you what happened to me, and to share my experience of cancer and my recovery.

Why? Because I know there are lots of people out there who have been given a death sentence, like I was and have been told, "There is no cure," or "There is nothing more we can do for you…There's no other viable treatment," and, of course, we believe what our doctors tell us.

Yet, in my instance, this was not the case.

For me, I know that it was my loving family, my friends, and my boyfriend at that time, my will to live, and my very special homoeopath, Janice, that saved my life.

In a nutshell, doctors in St Bartholomew's Hospital in London had diagnosed me with cancer. I had tumours in my brain and spine, and was given months to live. I had been given the usual treatments of chemotherapy and radiotherapy and various drugs from the doctors. My oncologist told me the treatment had not worked for me and I was given three alternatives before the inevitable happened:

Go to a hospice. We have a place booked for you.
Remain in the hospital.
Go home.

I chose to go home. But that all happened in 1996.

I am told that in all good speeches, books, essays, dissertations, research papers and things of such ilk, there should be a beginning, middle and an end. Well, in my case there is no end, or - at least - not the ending that we were expecting at that time. As I write this, I am in good health, very much alive and very happy to continue with my life.

I will tell you a little about my life before cancer. I will share with you the build up to finding out I was seriously ill, and being close to death. I will tell you my experience of the treatment I had from conventional medicine, and share with you my recovery from cancer.

I also want to explain a little about homoeopathy, the therapy that helped me. I want to do this because if you, or one of your siblings, your partner, your parents, your child or your friend, discovered they had a debilitating disease, a terminal illness, you'd want to help, wouldn't you?

If you were told there was nothing else the doctors could do, wouldn't you like hear about something else that might possibly help? About another option that just might help, even in the most, apparently, hopeless cases? I feel certain that it was homoeopathy that helped me. So maybe it could help you.

Understandably, I am eager to share my story and tell you about this amazing medicine which has been used for over 200 years: 200 years of experience, and with plenty of evidence and research to support it. And I will guide you to all this, and tell you about myself, and many people like me, who can testify to the empirical evidence that supports homoeopathy.

You may find this 1st chapter a bit discombobulated but that is just how I felt at the time when all this was happening – confused and frustrated, but here goes.

CHAPTER 1 - BEFORE CANCER

I was born at 8.30 am, Wednesday, 19 December, 1969. I am the last of seven children in my family and I was always told that this was significant when I was a child:- that it meant I would be lucky but those who have studied the astrology may know more about this.

As I have said, I had cancer and no ordinary cancer at that. I had cancer in the middle of my brain in the pineal gland, the one place where no surgeon can operate. It's just too awkward and a dangerous and potentially damaging place to do surgery, I was informed. Surgeons would have to cut through too many brain cells, which would cause too much damage. I was told that brain tumours, especially where my tumour was, were not that common but, since my recovery, I have heard more and more about their occurrence. I was also told I had a really rare type of tumour, normally only found in infant males - but I am an adult female, I can assure you.

WHEN I REALISED THERE WAS SOMETHING WRONG

The first inklings of something being wrong occurred when I was in my first real job. I was working as an admin assistant in a Staff Development Unit. It wasn't the job I wanted to do and I only got it because I'd been doing some temporary work there to tide me over after graduation. I had just finished a Social Science BA (Hons) degree at Wolverhampton Polytechnic and I needed to pay back my student loan and the money that the bank had lent me. So I got the first available job to remove some of the weight and worry I had about my overdraft.

I had found my degree in Social Science very interesting, definitely my kind of thing, but I was soon to find out in the job market, my BA degree seemed to stand for "Bugger All." I was cross that my degree seemed worthless to employers. On more than one occasion during the job-hunting process, I thought about how I could have left school at sixteen and trained myself to do something more practical and vocational.

It was 1991 and jobs were scarce for graduates. I had wanted, maybe in my innocence, to find a job to invoke peace, justice, equality and fairness to all. So, whilst looking for my real job, my true vocation, I decided to learn to type in order to do temporary work in administration. I eventually found a temporary position and the administrator manager, Shirley, suggested that I could stay on full-time. They needed someone permanent as the office was incredibly busy. In my opinion, they needed at least two new people for the position. I had just done a degree and I did not want to be on the lowest rung in an office, but I responded enthusiastically; the bottom line was that I needed a job and some money! The possibility of a contract and the security that that brings with it was important.

Yet, time went by and no contract or permanent post had actually been offered. I stayed there without any sick pay or holiday pay, and there seemed to be so many Bank Holidays, for which of course I was not paid.

A colleague suggested that I should maybe take a few odd days off - to have some 'make-believe' interviews. Perhaps this would hurry them up a bit - I didn't want to be dishonest and certainly didn't feel in a position to do that. I had been applying for jobs on a regular basis and, as luck would have it, I got a positive reply from one of my application forms for a Building Society. A graduate position and a proper job, with training. An interview was booked.

Working for a Building Society certainly wasn't the job I had wanted to do and I definitely hadn't wanted a job with any financial aspect to it. I'd just stopped being a student; it was the '80s and a dog-eat-dog, materialistic world. Mrs. Thatcher was in office and I was anti all things capitalistic but, when I was invited for an interview, I was shocked to find that I was secretly quite proud of myself! I was really pleased to get any interview. I felt oh-so-cocky when I announced to my boss that I would be having an interview with a Building Society and so must take a half-day off work. I slipped into the conversation the amount of money they were prepared to pay for me, which was actually a great deal more than they were planning to offer me.

I made it plain, without actually saying so, that if they didn't get their act together, then I may well have to leave and go elsewhere.

On hearing this they swooped in and offered me a contract at long last, albeit only for 6 months. What this actually meant to me was that I could take a few days off, celebrate, go down to

Glastonbury Festival and actually get paid for doing it. Splendid! What more could I ask for?

I love Glastonbury Festival; it's just fab. Everybody is in such a good mood. Some of my best moments have been spent there. My favourite bands, loads of interesting stores selling jewellery, Indian wall-hangings and a huge variety of different cuisine. This is one place, where being a vegetarian is no problem. They have all sorts of different types of people, leading an alternative life and I couldn't help but look at them enviously. I felt that my life and job were so mundane and monotonous. I wanted to be more alternative, to be out there pushing to 'Help the Environment', to 'Ban the Bomb', to encourage people not to wear fur coats, and so on.

Anyway, it wasn't too long after getting my new post when I began to experience odd moments of dizziness and flashing lights once or twice a day, every few days. I had an eye test and was told that my eyesight was perfect although I would probably need reading glasses by the time I was 40. The optician's receptionist suggested it might be because of my vegetarian diet. Not getting enough vitamin B12 most likely. This theory supported all my dad's theories on vegetarianism. I was irritated by this suggestion and felt certain that this was not the cause of my problems. So I went to my doctor - his investigation found I had a slightly lower than average sugar level in my blood and a low potassium level. I asked what things have potassium in. Coconut was the answer. So I said, thinking what had sugar and coconut in, "Does this mean that I should eat Bounty Bars from now on?"

He said that if I wanted to, I could. So this gave me leave to eat chocolate. Yum ... one of my favourite pastimes!

Can you believe it, a doctor telling me to eat chocolate bars! Well, I did just that but, not surprisingly, my eyes were still not right so I returned to the doctor, as requested, when there had been no improvement and I was sent to an Eye Out-Patients at the local hospital where I was to see a specialist. They called to make me an appointment but no-one at the hospital could see me, they were too busy.

Following the non-appointment, I returned to work and it was just about the most hectic day there. But deadlines were deadlines. I told my colleague, Shirley, what had happened and she went immediately to the Personnel Department and arranged for me to see the Company doctor straight away. So off

I went again. As luck would have it, he had specialised in neurology. He was the first one to see from looking at my eyes that something was seriously wrong.

I think, in order not to worry me, he didn't tell me everything he surmised and told me to get a taxi and go directly to Accident and Emergency at St Bart's Hospital and to take with me this letter he had written. I was to stay there until I was seen. He told me to expect a long wait. It was!

After numerous probing questions I found myself being taken to have a CAT scan for my head. I didn't know what this was or what it was for really. The nurse got me into a wheelchair. I was thinking, why do I need a wheelchair? Regardless, I played patient and remember complimenting her and remarked that "This is really good service." It was then midnight and I remember thinking how great it was that they were still doing scans at that time of night. The nurse told me that they didn't usually do this and they had put the scanner into operation especially for me. They only ever did this for severe car accidents, and usually the patient isn't conscious, so this was quite unusual. All I could think was, "So what am I doing here then?"

They put me in the scanner. I had only seen equipment like this on TV, when they were doing a documentary on cancer patients. I felt sure that I didn't have that. I only had a few flashing lights now and again, no pain or anything but of course, this thought had raced through my mind, momentarily.

I told myself not to be silly and to stop being a hypochondriac.

We got back to the Outpatients, where I followed the doctors down the corridor, as they were going to discuss my scan with two other doctors. They huddled together and spoke softly. I couldn't hear what they were saying and it dawned on me that maybe they didn't want me there. I said, "Shall I sit over there?" pointing to my outpatient curtained cubical. They looked horrified that I was behind them. They hadn't realized that I was there. I felt pretty furious that they were not involving me in their discussion; it was my head they were talking about, after all!

It was 2.00-am at that point and they suggested I stayed in the hospital for the night, rather than go home. I lived over the other side of London and the Tubes had stopped at that hour anyway.

They found me a bed straight away. "Funny," I thought. "Maybe the Conservatives, at that time, had been right and we don't have a problem with bed shortages in the NHS after all."

A GLOOMY NIGHT

I arrived at my abode for the night. I didn't have a tooth brush with me, of course, and they had run out but they did give me a lovely flowery, nylon nightie with a slit up the back of it. As I lay in my bed I pondered over what had happened. It was dark and all the other patients were sleeping and snoring except one young woman. She was about my age and was watching TV with headphones on. She came over and asked why I was here. All I could say was that I'd been told I had something wrong with my head but I don't know what.

I suspected something was not right: an available bed, the scanner being opened especially at midnight and their readiness to help me out by having me stay there overnight. I didn't want to wake any of the other patients so I went into a rather smelly toilet to cry my eyes out. It wasn't until the next morning that I found out I'd gone to the men's toilets by mistake!

After little sleep, I was desperate to phone my mum and tell her where I was. She lived in the West Midlands where I had grown-up. I asked a nurse to wheel the portable phone over. She suggested that I leave it a little while longer. It was only 5.30 am. I did, I waited impatiently until 6.30 am. My parents are the sort who were always up early, making cups of tea, and saying their morning prayers.

My sister Antonia (my family call her Toe) happened to be staying for the weekend at our parents' so she and my mother hot-footed it down to London straight away.

I was so delighted when they appeared. My sister came rushing up and we held onto each other as if we were clams. I guess she suspected the worst but couldn't say it.

It was a Friday night when I was admitted and the specialists don't work at the weekend, so I had to wait until Monday for news on my scans.

"I could have gone home for the weekend after all, unless they were afraid that something dreadful would happen to me."

THE RESULTS

When they arrived, the medical results showed I had hydrocephalus, a condition that children usually get. It is more commonly known as 'water on the brain'. This is when there is a build-up of fluid in your head due to a tube in your head narrowing or some sort of blockage, a tumour perhaps. Either way, I was to have brain surgery. A shunt, a tube running from my brain to my intestines, would be inserted, to drain away the cerebral fluid that usually flowed around my brain freely.

The prospect of brain surgery sounded scary but I was reassured that this was a relatively easy neurological operation so it didn't alarm me too much. It seemed like an easy solution - one tube doesn't work, so you put another in to do the job instead - easy. The operation took place as soon as possible. No waiting list for me, even though I'd been told it wasn't all that urgent. I was told later that I could have lost my eyesight if I had waited any longer.

THE OPERATION

To perform this operation, they were going to have to shave a small channel of my hair off, from over my ear but this was only going to be about an inch wide and it would grow back. Initially, I wondered what all the fuss was about but I was to find out later.

The next day, after the operation, the same doctor came up to see me and said he had a confession to make, that they had had to shave half of my hair off. This was the least of my worries. What choice did I really have? OK, I'd lost half my hair to have an operation but the alternative could have been massively worse, even fatal.

As luck would have it, my hair was thick and shoulder length, so I successfully hid my baldness by parting the side of head that had hair and pulling it over to the other side; a sort of Bobby Charlton style. This, coupled with wide headscarves, solved any embarrassment. I was surprised at my concern over my hair. I don't consider myself to be particularly self-conscious but a trip, later to the hairdresser, proved me to be wrong.

About six months after all this, my hair had grown a few inches and I went to see if they could even it up a bit and get some sort of style out of it. I thought of myself as quite a confident person. I'm not one to just agree that a horrific hair cut is fine to the hairdresser. I sat there and I had to unwind my headscarf and reveal my secret and looking in the mirror with one side of my hair long, the other short. I was so embarrassed I just felt so exposed. My face went really red, my voice went all croaky. I told myself that this was ridiculous, that she was just a hairdresser that I'd never meet or see again. So what was my problem?

Prior to this, whilst in hospital after my operation, the wig man visited me. I didn't expect him. He just turned up beside my hospital bed, with a brown suitcase, full of wigs. I was asked if I wanted to try some on. There were some long blond curly ones, some short grey curly ones, some red, some black; all he could stuff inside a small case. I could choose any of these or chose one from a picture he'd brought with him. I really was not bothered with them and somewhat embarrassed by it. Had it not been for my persistent mother, who was visiting at the time, I would have sent him and his bag, packing. She convinced me that I may want one at a later date and anyway, why not have one, they were free. So I decided not to go for a colour change or a curl or even a different length. I chose the very same style and colour I had had pre-operation, a dark brown pageboy bob, as I liked my hair that way.

So I became a wig owner, but my pride would not allow me to wear it and I stuck to my scarves. The wig did serve to be very therapeutic, in a different way. I got people I thought would never try it on to wear it: my dad, my brother in law and even my 88 year-old grandmother who, to our amusement, looked like the woman from the Planet of the Apes! It is astonishing what people will do if you are ill. We all had so much fun with it. Everyone was up for a laugh.

As the news about me being in hospital spread, I had more and more visitors. It was just great to have so many. I was told at one point that I had to go to a separate side room with my visitors, as there were too many of them and we were making too much noise, I guess.

I had thirteen different visitors at the same time at one point - It was great, just like a big reunion. I loved it because I'd thought of myself more as an only child because, although I had six brothers and sisters. I was the baby and the age gap between my next sibling and myself was nearly seven years. They started to leave home when I was around six and by the age of thirteen I was on my own. Two of my sisters had emigrated to South Africa and one had gone with her husband to America. Also, I'd been sent to a private school on the other side the city and as I'd gone to a school that was not local to where we lived, my friends lived all over the West Midlands. This meant I rarely saw them outside school. I was conscious of people calling me names like "posh!" or "spoilt!" because of the school I'd been sent to. I was lacking in self-confidence but when I went to Polytechnic, I came out of my shell and made many good friends. Later on, when I became ill, it was so important for me to have their support. It was a shame that it had to be under these circumstances.

During that first weekend at hospital, I had so many phone calls too. My sisters abroad were concerned for me and would call me from South Africa and America. I'd barely start a conversation with a visitor and the ward phone would ring for me.

Late one night, after what became three weeks in hospital, I counted that I had had over fifty different visitors, many of whom came more than once. One friend, Dominic, who worked nearby, visited three times a day; once before work, in his dinner hour and then after work. Being in hospital was so dismal it was lovely to get regular visits throughout the day. You find that some people just shine through in these situations. People, who you wouldn't expect to visit arrived and expressed such unconditional positive regard for me and my health, I will always be grateful to those people who came to see me then.

While I recovered from my operation the doctors told me, with absolute certainty, that I did not have a tumour. Nothing had shown up on their scanners to lead them to say I had. One of the tubes in my head must have just narrowed, by itself, for no known reason.

I was shocked. I didn't know they were looking for a tumour. I told my dad and he seem very relieved. I was shocked again. Had he also thought I might have a tumour too?? To everybody's relief, it had all just been a peculiar quirk of nature: - my tubes had narrowed. After recuperation at my parents' house, I was eager to return to my usual life in London and returned to my job.

At this point, my hair had not grown back properly and so I had to continue to wear my headscarf. This did not match their corporate image at all. Although they didn't insist on me wearing a grey shoulder-padded suit, I did feel they weren't too happy about what I think they felt was a hippy, headscarf! I had no hair but I did have a contract. But this was to run out shortly and they offered me a new one - for one month. Yes, one month!

I suppose they didn't want to be stuck with me if I got ill again. I resumed work, and I was doing my best, which they had deemed to be good enough before, as they had made me a job offer. Since I had been away there seemed to have been many changes going on within the department and it just seemed like I couldn't keep up. Nothing was explained to me. They just expected me to know it all without explaining anything to me. Mistakes were being made and I seemed to be the one they put the blame on. This didn't seem fair and they got impatient with me when I asked questions, or referred telephone calls to them regarding queries that they felt I should know about - even though I had never been told. On reflection, I can now appreciate that I may have been told but my memory couldn't retain it.

The worst error I made was when a workshop for 80 or so teachers had been arranged. Amongst other things, I was to make sure all the files and papers for each participant to receive, were sent to the required locations. These would be vital to the day's workshop. On this particular occasion, I arranged that the correct number of boxes of files were sent to a planned venue but I heard a week or so later that I had sent the wrong set of files to the workshop. My boss was on his own in the office whilst I and the other administrative staff were away helping at conferences. He had to spend all morning ringing round to double check if they had taken the wrong boxes only to find that this was not the case and they had taken the ones I had told them to transport. Chasing all this up would have taken him all morning; it had to be sorted immediately and he was the only one there to do it. What a pickle he must have been in. Eighty rather agitated teachers who had come from all over the country and taken days off work, waiting for their workshop files. My boss must have thought I had done it on purpose, especially as the timing was so right, him being in the office all by himself was an unusual event.

I had felt angry with my employer about only being given a month's contract, although, of course, I had said nothing. I couldn't have planned a better revenge if I had tried! But I hadn't. The outcome was that they took me aside, pointed out to me that I wasn't as sharp as I used to be and that they would not be renewing my contract.

By now my debts had been paid and I would get my month's salary when I left work. So I decided to make something positive out of the situation - make it into a blessing in disguise. Rather than look for another job straight off, I would go travelling first, something I'd always wanted to do but had never had enough money. I decided that I would work as I travelled.

I chose to go to a Kibbutz, something I had heard about only briefly. It would be perfect. I could work in a socialist environment where everyone did everything and where there are no hierarchies. Why not live there for a while, rather than here? I could see some of the country, meet some fellow Kibbutznicks and travel to Egypt and Jordan; see the Pyramids, travel on the Nile; go to the Pink City in Jordan, across the desert on a camel. "So yes," I thought, "that is what I shall do."

MY SPONTANEOUS ADVENTURE

OK, maybe living in a kibbutz is hardly a socialist statement but it was as near as I felt I could make it. I booked it up, leased my room in London, and stored all my belongings. I even learned a few words of Hebrew. I packed my borrowed rucksack and stayed at my friend's flat the day before I left. Sue, my friend, was at work and I had a day to spare but that morning I got out of the bath and felt dizzy. I could see flashing lights! Alarm bells went off. "Is my shunt working properly?" I had been told it could fail on me. The doctor had likened it to a car: some last for years without any trouble, others always seem to be going wrong.

I panicked. What if I went to Israel regardless and I got worse? Do they have the same kind of shunt there as they do here? I had a special type, one where the valve in my head could be changed from the outside with a magnetic device to let fluid flow around my head at the correct setting. Clever, but did they have the correct, up-to-date equipment in Israel? I didn't want an emergency operation all those miles away, in a strange country. I phoned the hydrocephalus help-line and they put me in contact with one of the doctors who worked for them and often did special talks on hydrocephalus. He suggested that I be cautious and stay in the UK. I was also told that I might also get too hot working in such a country and get dehydrated, not something a person with hydrocephalus should ever risk. He recommended that I should get myself checked over first.

I was not foolish. I was having dizzy spells and a doctor was advising me to stay, so I did. I phoned the Kibbutz agent and cancelled. I cried and cried in disappointment. This was to have been my big adventure and all my hopes and wishes had been dashed with that one call. That evening, I had planned to meet a crowd of my friends in a pub, who were sending me off. I just couldn't make it. I was too sad. One of my close friends then came round with the presents people had bought me to go off with. How lovely, but oh, how sad did I feel. So I was left jobless, homeless, with only a rucksack full of clothes, my dreams broken, my boyfriend, of two years had recently broken up with me and this looming fear that there might be something going wrong in my head again.

I had contacted the hospital to tell them of my concerns. They took a head scan immediately and I went to get the results a few days later. The consultant said, "Been getting afraid of going to

Israel, have we?" in a most patronising manner. I was furious with his reaction. I had no abnormalities on my scan and so he presumed I had made it all up. Their scanners showed nothing but I know how it feels when something in that part of my brain is out of sorts.

I was relieved that the scan showed nothing but I was not satisfied with his conclusions. I knew there was something wrong and I told him not to be so patronising. I was furious.

I had lost all the money that I had spent on the planned trip to Israel, and had very little money left. My sister in America called and invited me to visit there instead. I leapt at the chance. I had never wanted to go to America. I didn't want to go anywhere 'westernised'. I wanted a complete change of culture but the American option was safe, they had a hospital nearby, and my sister had found out that they knew about my type of shunt. I decided I would go and I would leave the very next day. How great it was to say to her on the phone, "I'm coming across the Atlantic Ocean to see you for six weeks and I am coming tomorrow." I loved the impetuous nature of it all and the flexibility I had.

I had the best time. My sister Judith is thirteen years my senior. She left our family house when I was only about six years old. I'd seen her now and again, but we really didn't know each other that well. I wondered how she felt about her young sister landing upon her for, not two weeks, not three weeks but six?

We all had a great time, my sister, her husband, Syd, and my three nephews, Jonathan, Adam and Thomas. One event we did that stands clearly in my mind, was our trip to Niagara Falls. It was nothing less than amazing! As I gazed upon the Falls, I made sure that I took it all in as I recalled the fact that I may have gone blind if I hadn't alerted the doctors of my problems.

When my holiday ended, I returned to England and moved in with some friends to busy, bustling Brixton. It was lively and energetic, humming with buskers, drunkards, flower and fruit stalls and people hounding you to give them your tube ticket, once finished with. Going through the barriers, you'd find people would run up close to you as you went through, so they too could get through the barriers with you without paying, and then hurtle down the left-hand side of the escalators. The left hand of the escalators are always left empty so commuters can rush about like scalded cats and get to their destination, ooh, five minutes earlier.

So, there I was in Brixton sharing a house with my two friends I'd known from Polytechnic and one other friend of theirs. I got a new job at an Art and Design college. I was to arrange short and evening art courses. This was OK, a little boring though, as there didn't seem to be too many people doing evening courses in art and design at the time. Some days I had one booking to administer all day. I'd fill my days with watering the potted plants.

Meanwhile, my hair had grown a little so I could dispense with the headscarves. I could turn my head and let my hair swing from one side to another - a favoured movement I had on the dance floor. I loved to go out dancing. It was at my favourite club that I met Allan.

One particular night a guy – Allan - had caught my eye, we danced and then we kissed. At the very same moment, my friend, Sue, had also met someone. At the end of the night, we exchanged phone numbers. I didn't want any of this "I'll phone you" and then you're left waiting for the phone to ring and when they don't call back, periodically checking whether the phone is working or not. No, I would have his number too, should I decide to contact him again.

He called me the very next day and we'd meet regularly to go a comedy club, or see the latest films on the big screens in Piccadilly Circus and then to China Town to a Chinese restaurant. Our relationship developed and I was very happy but sometimes strange symptoms were happening. They didn't worry me but, looking back, they were signs that something was wrong.

For example, my memory seemed to let me down more and more frequently. It was early on in our relationship; I was cooking tea and Allan turned up at my door at about 6.30pm after work. "How lovely" I thought, what a surprise and I asked him what he was doing here. Apparently, I'd asked him to dinner! I'd totally forgotten! A mistake anyone could make but I made it more than once and not just with Allan.

Previously, my friend phoned and asked, "Where are you?" I was half an hour late for her dinner. I didn't think, "Oh God! I forgot!" or "Oops, my mistake." I simply denied making any such plans.

I discovered that if you have a real memory problem, then you don't remember you have a memory problem! Things don't come back in a flash. I'd have to discuss the matter for ten or so minutes before I could maybe recall any such conversation. It's not like forgetting where you have put your glasses or keys. As far as I was concerned that arrangement had not been made!

Gradually, as good friends and family pointed my problem out, I'd simply had to reconsider my situation; "Why would so many beloved dear friends and family be so awkward about things?" I began to think this was something more sinister. I took to writing everything down, every date and arrangement.

My friends were very patient but work was not. My manager would get frustrated with me forgetting to give her important messages and memos. I was left feeling very stupid and incapable. They simply didn't understand that I wasn't a dizzy and disorganized young woman. It wasn't fair, because this simply wasn't me - except it was!

Around this time, I had intermittent consultations with the neurologist and neurosurgeons. On one particular occasion, I went alone to see my neurosurgeons because I had gone completely do-lally after having a bit too much to drink. I had been wary about having too much alcohol, as I knew it affected your brain. I was particularly worried it would affect my shunt and was told by a neurosurgeon to take it easy, only one glass now and again if I wanted, but on another occasion, I was told by another that there shouldn't be any additional danger in having a few drinks. I tried it out; I had a few more than I would normally since my operation but a whole lot less than I would have previously.

On this occasion, I went out dancing and had a drink or two but I remembered very little of the next three days. I was told I was sick all over Sue's bedroom carpet, and had slept and slept, so that she could hardly wake me and she was concerned about getting to work the following day.

I recall being told that I had problems waking. If I was tired, nothing and nobody could wake me. The lads in my house told me I fell asleep on my sofa once and they tried to waken me, pushed the sofa around the room and shouted at me but to no avail.
Sue had managed to put me in a taxi and phoned my housemates to warn them of my arrival. On my way home, I apparently stopped off at a cash point to get some money to pay

the driver. I could swear that this did not happen but later I found I had a receipt for it in my coat pocket. Apparently, I was also sick in the taxi. This was a whole 24 hours after drinking and I really hadn't had that much to drink.

Hearing about this my sister called my flat mate and urged him to take me to Casualty. We were in the taxi going there and he told me that I kept asking the same questions over and over again. "So, where are we going then? What time is it?" I got to Casualty and we waited there for hours and hours. Apparently, Allan too had been redirected from my house to hospital when we had planned to meet. He had told me I was lying on a stretcher, being asked the very easy questions that nurses ask patients, to test their awareness. "What's your name?", "Where are you?" and "Who is the Prime Minister?"

I got none of these correct.

These kinds of errors happened irregularly and sometimes I was fine and other times not Allan told me about this years later but, to me, everything had seemed fine. For instance, on another occasion I'd set my radio alarm clock for work for the morning and had set it to play on the loudest volume for up to an hour. I didn't hear it, which would make me late for work. My sister was getting more and more concerned and would ring me more than usual.

I felt she seemed to be the only one who recognised there was a real, possible, medical problem. I hadn't just experienced a bad hangover. She had noticed on other occasions I couldn't even answer simple questions like what day was it, etc. I was angry with her because I thought everyone forgets what day it is now and again, don't they? Previously, she had asked me for my home address, she hadn't noted it in her address book. I'd been living there for three or four months now but I couldn't remember it! I had to go outside to the front of the house and check the number on the door.

This kind of thing was happening more and more. My work colleagues were astounded when I announced that I now knew my boyfriend's telephone number. I was feeling pretty good about this new achievement. They looked at me horrified.
"How long have you been seeing him now?"
"Do you know our work's number?"
"No."
"Do you know the fax number?"

"Of course not."

This really upset me. I could always look it up if asked by an inquirer on the phone. I didn't need to know our fax number, or our telephone number. What a waste of energy that would be, I hardly knew my own telephone number let alone the work's number!

Getting back to the hospital, the staff, when I went to Casualty, had made an appointment for me with a neurologist. My sister came over from Cardiff especially to be with me at the appointment, to put her view across, to help me remember too, and to ensure I wrote down everything I needed to tell him and ask him. She knows about these things - she is a clinical psychologist.

The neurologist listened to what we had to say, looked at his CT scan of my brain and seeing no anomalies said to me, "You are either mad, taking drugs or we have missed something." He then told us that he would arrange for me to see a psychiatrist. I guess he thought I must be mad! My sister was furious, knowing that I was not mad and I was not taking drugs. Personally, I was just happy that something was going to be done. Tonia told him that she thought they had missed something and after we left his consultation room she urged me to contact my GP.

I did just that and some weeks later I was referred to Kings College Hospital to see a neurologist. He agreed that there was something wrong and he sent me for an MRI scan. I was also sent to see a psychologist, who confirmed that I had some damage to my left and right brain lobes; minor damage, but enough to cause memory problems. So, I wasn't mad and I wasn't a hysterical hypochondriac young woman who created symptoms but someone with a real, physical problem!

I visited a consultant neurologist and he saw, after studying my scans, that there was a mass. As a result of my appointment in December 1995 I had a more intense, deeper scan called a gadolinium scan. This is where they inject radioactive ink into your blood to highlight if anything abnormal is going on. I was to await the results of my MRI scan.

Weeks passed. I was anxious to learn of their findings. Had I got something awful going on in my brain or not? I telephoned the hospital but I just couldn't get any information from the neurologist. When I finally got through, I was told not to bother him!

Bother him? Didn't they realise the importance of this? There was something wrong with my brain! I was advised to contact my GP. She would have the letter with my scan results. So, my neurologist did have the information. I was cross that he hadn't contacted me. I made an appointment with my GP. She found the letter amongst my huge pile of notes. She read them, as if for the first time. Hadn't she read her post before it had been filed away? Anyway, as she read her eyes widened and she looked concerned. She said that I should wait for my appointment from the hospital, but I wanted to know what the letter said NOW. I had hung about for appointments before, for too long.

She seemed very reluctant to tell me what it said. I knew I could demand to see my doctor's notes and I urged her further. She said that I might need a stereotactic biopsy. I had no idea what that meant. She said that she didn't know what it was either and that she would contact my neurologist about this so come back next week, when she had done this.

There was no way that I could wait a week to find out. I had been told I might need a stereotactic biopsy. I needed to know right NOW exactly what that meant. Why couldn't she call him up right away, why wait until next week?

I had no idea what a biopsy was let alone a stereotactic biopsy was. This was before the common use of the world wide web and Google. I decided that I would telephone the neurosurgeon myself.

This turned out to be problematic for a number of reasons: I worked the same hours as the neurosurgeon and I did not want to call him whilst I was at work. This was the pre-mobile phone and Internet era so I had to go and find a telephone box in my lunch hour. The neurosurgeon was never in. I left messages for him to phone me, at the Out Patients, with his secretary, at Kings College Hospital and the other Hospital, the Maudsley. Finally, he returned my call one evening when I was at home. He said that from my scan, he could see a few small tumours.

A FEW SMALL TUMOURS???? TUMOURS...... A FEW.

He continued and said he may have to take a biopsy to see exactly what was going on. But what did stereotactic mean? I asked. He told me that he would explain that when I saw him. I was to wait for an appointment to come through the post. He wasn't sure when that would be but that I was to wait until then.

I WAS DEVASTATED. I sat on my stairs in my house by the phone. I phoned my boyfriend, Allan - he was out. I phoned my mum and dad - they were out. I phoned my sister in Cardiff, Tonia, only to find that she was also out. The worst HAD actually happened. I had only fleetingly thought about having a tumour. I had told myself not to be so silly, not to make a mountain out of a molehill. I shook with fear. I phoned constantly for two and a half-hours trying to contact someone who'd listen. But nobody was in.

Finally, I got through to Tonia. She asked if there was anyone in my house who I could talk to. There wasn't, but I did eventually get through to Allan and asked him to come over. The London tubes had stopped running, and the night buses were infrequent, and not direct. So I offered to pay for a taxi and asked him to come over immediately. He did, he stayed all night, and held me tight.

It was some weeks later that my promised appointment came through. They didn't demand to see me immediately - so not that urgent or dangerous then? Just a few small brain tumours. How long or how bad did things have to get before I got their attention?

When eventually the appointment date came, Allan accompanied me. Going to the outpatients was quite a relief. I trusted this neurologist. He had accepted something was wrong. He had listened to me and I felt really reassured by him. Finally, I thought, they would be able to clear it all up and get things sorted. But when we arrived at Outpatients I was told my neurologist had retired! I was to see another neurologist who, I was to find out, knew nothing about my case.

As the new neurologist looked at my MRI scan, he told me that I had one tumour. When I informed him that I had been told I had a few tumours, he was emphatic - I only had one.

I was relieved. My new neurologist seemed good and was quite reassuring, so I put my trust in him. I was to go back for a checkup in a few months' time. However, when I returned for my next appointment, I had to see another person, this time a trainee neurologist. So again, I had to explain all my symptoms from the beginning, as she wasn't familiar with my case.

Alongside all of this and before I was told I had a tumour, I had been seeing an eye specialist since I had hydrocephalus. My eyesight was damaged. I had double vision, but strangely just around the perimeter of my eyesight. I had several appointments at the hospital and they really weren't too sure why I had a problem with my eyes. They had been told that I had not got a tumour.

My eyesight had varied over the years. At first, I had had flashing lights before I had my hydrocephalus operation. I could still read and use a computer for work. Sometimes I would hardly notice it. But at other times the double vision would encroach alarmingly close towards my central vision then go back to normal again.

For a while, things stabilised and I could go to work ok. I had moved out of my house in Brixton and into a house in West Norwood with my cousin and her friend. West Norwood had no underground. It was an hour and a half to my boyfriend's house, and any of my friends. I felt really quite isolated there. Whilst living at this house I had a sickness bug. I worried about this, as I knew that sickness was the first sign of my shunt not working. I was frightened that the fluid in my head would build up; I would fall into unconsciousness, collapse and die. Of course, it could also just be a sickness bug but what if it wasn't! Often, my cousin was out and my other housemate, Emma, a nurse, was on duty. I could die there and no one would know. I phoned my sister, Tonia, and told her to ask me simple memory questions, to make sure I was still compos mentis. I was. She promised to call me in the morning and check me out again. She did and it was a huge relief to find I got all the questions right.

I had only been living there for six months when Emma decided to go travelling, so we needed to find someone else to replace her or move out completely. My friend, Kate, knew of a room in a large Victorian house in North London. I was to share with four other women; it was only three-quarters of an hour's bus journey away from work and fifteen minutes bus journey from Allan's. It had a cat, a real Victorian wood burning fireplace, a garden, a double room and cost less than where I was living. It sounded like a much better option for me.

I was happier with my house but I hated my job intensely and continually complained about it. This prompted me to do an evening course in counselling skills. I thought this would be a good distraction and something else to do in my now seemingly mundane life. It was also something that I had considered doing after my degree. It seemed to be the obvious choice and would marry up with my social science degree. I hoped it would put me on the right career path but the information I received about the course had, at that time, said I had to be a lot older. I was only in my early twenties. However, years later, my desire to be a counsellor remained.

I'll never forget the first class. There were about 20 of us. We had to go into pairs and tell the other person five things we liked about ourselves and five things we disliked about ourselves. "Oh my God!" Panic.
Five things I liked about myself. Well, maybe I could think of one or maybe two - but I certainly couldn't tell anyone else what I thought they were. This was too embarrassing. It would be conceited of me to say I liked things about myself! So I sat there and I just couldn't come up with anything to say, which made it even more embarrassing because it made me feel pathetic and too modest.

Despite that first challenge, as the course progressed, I loved it and warmed to having to look into myself and others. I had a taste for it and, once I completed the course, I started to do voluntary work at Drink Line. This provides information and counselling skills on the telephone line for people with drink problems. This was much more my sort of thing and no administration!

Inspired, I looked at doing a Diploma Course. I would have to go to work full time and do the course at the same time in order to pay for it. I would also have to be counselled myself, do some voluntary counselling, as well as studying for the course, and attending one full day at college. I wanted to do it so much but I couldn't afford to do it in terms of time, energy or finance. I was frustrated. I had finally found something I really wanted to do, but I couldn't do it.

However, I did manage to change my job to cover a maternity leave at a different art college. It was a college registrar's post. This would be a step up and a move away from my nightmare manager. I also managed to get some more training for voluntary, face-to-face counselling at another local alcohol unit. This voluntary work would at least move me in the right direction.

Meanwhile, I was getting peculiar feelings in my head, the odd dizzy spell. I felt really stressed and worried about it all - I was fed up with the restriction I now had following my hydrocephalus. I couldn't just go out and have a drink. People didn't seem to appreciate my anger and loss. I felt ashamed that I had such a problem with it. Surely, I could find better things to do and different ways to socialise but it seemed really hard to me.

I turned to BACUP, a cancer support organisation, now merged with Macmillan Cancer Support. They offer free counselling for cancer sufferers. I had not been told I had cancer, all I knew at this point was that I had a few tumours in my head. I didn't feel like it was exactly the right place for me, I felt guilty being there. I was taking up the place of someone else, who actually DID have cancer. I worried that I was 'talking myself' into getting cancer; I had a brain tumour, not cancer but I didn't know of anywhere to go to for counselling for my problem. I didn't seem to fit anyone's criteria.

I started to need to take taxis there from my house in Islington to the nearest BAC centre in Old Street, as my head was getting worse. My vision was really peculiar. It looked like the pavement was moving as I walked down the street. It was hard to go into shops as this was just too visually stimulating - too many things, too many colours - it made my stomach churn. I would feel sick and unsteady. My head would feel like it was being squashed.

As my memory got worse, I can only roughly outline the order of events that followed. I went to see my neurosurgeon with my sister Judith, recently returned from the US, who had come down again to London specially to support me. I went to get my MRI scan results to find out if my tumours had grown. So it was yet another anxious, worrying time. Judith dressed up, smart, glasses on, notebook in hand; she looked rather official. Judith had been mistaken for my mother at previous appointments but this time she looked very professional. She could have been another doctor, a reporter, or a social worker. On several occasions the doctors had not got my medical notes at my appointment. He would need to have my notes in front of him now.

We had waited in the waiting room for one and a half hours only to discover that he didn't have my notes, again! He quickly picked up the phone and demanded that they be brought to him. Eventually, he got my records and spoke to my sister about me about the results, not once glancing at me. I was furious. "You can speak to me," I told him. I'd heard of this kind of treatment from doctors before but this was the late 20th century. I was the patient, an adult. He was talking about MY brain, MY tumour but not to me!

He showed us the recent MRI which, to my horror, showed that the tumour had grown significantly! He then said that we should do something about this and confirmed that a biopsy was needed. I was astounded. I stopped him. "Look, I know I've been pushing for something to be done about all of this but I don't want you to do anything unnecessary because I've been too persistent".

He was adamant: it was now necessary to have a biopsy but first they had to get some of my fluid from the shunt in my head to ascertain what sort of tumour it was. He explained that I needed to have a needle in my head in my shunt to extract some of the fluid from it for it to be examined. First, he would have to shave a little of my hair for this to happen.

Suddenly I felt that things were happening too fast. There and then he produced a razor blade and to me he seemed to swish it around the room as if he were a Chinese warrior and shaved a section of my hair from my scalp - such sudden action! I hadn't expected it. I wanted him to go back to his previous inaction. He explained that his colleague would actually be doing the extracting of the cerebral fluid so we were ushered to another room to wait for him.

"Does mum want to stay with you?" asked the nurse.

Judith had got quite irritated by these sorts of comments by now. I retorted, "Yes, she does". Just as a joke between Judith and me.

In walked the colleague.

I was startled.

Of all the people in the world I didn't want to be putting a needle in my head, it was him.

Chapter 2 - The Biopsy

JANUARY 1996

So there I was, confronted with HIM again and his needle.
I'd lost trust in him and his ability as a doctor and was anxious about seeing him again. You see, I had met this doctor previously when going to an outpatient's appointment. It was just a check-up, so I didn't feel I needed anyone with me. He was at his desk - another new face for me at the time; another doctor who knew nothing about my case. I waited to see him for an hour or more, although I was there promptly for the appointment. He opened a green card folder, which would contain my notes but it only had one blank piece of paper.
"What is your address?" he asked.

I knew my files were in more than one folder, as they had already completely filled one folder. They were bulky. Why didn't he have them? How could he possibly be of any use if he knew nothing about me and had no information to hand, on me? For God's sake, he didn't even have my address! Did I really have to go through all the details of my illness all over again?

"My address is in my notes. Where are they?" I asked with some indignation.
How could I trust these people? They couldn't organise a piss-up in a brewery, as they say in the Black Country. I refused to give

him my details and told him to find the notes. I was furious! He sent me back into the waiting room while he located the scans. I was shaking with anger. Such incompetence!

After another long wait, I was summoned again. He had looked at my scans.
"You know it's probably cancer, don't you? You'll be seeing a neurosurgeon for the rest of your life."

Well, that's a nice way to tell someone they've got cancer isn't it. Not "Have you anyone with you to help you deal with this information?" or "We'll do something about this"; not even "I'll send you for tests to see if it is definitely cancer." Just, it's 'probably' cancer. I wanted to **know** if it was cancer.

He sent me off saying, "We'll send you an out-patients appointment shortly." Like that ever happened I thought! Shortly -when would this happen?
What was I to do? I'd just been told I might have cancer.
I was on my own.
I was supposed to be going back to work.
I could hardly breathe. My chest felt heavy, my eyes welled up.
I had to cross London to get back to work.

I waited at the station for the train into Victoria. Beside me, a mother and her child were also waiting; I sat on the steps watching them. I've never wanted kids, but this little one looked so pretty and was so well-behaved and chatting to her mum. How could I even hope to have children now I might have cancer? It wouldn't be fair to a baby to pass it on. Being faced with the harsh reality that I probably couldn't, brought on the urge to want one and also the grief of not being able to have one. I sat on the station stairs, head in hands, gulping for air, every breath hurting my chest.

On my way home, I decided to go and see my cousin Elaine who worked at Next, the clothes shop, in Victoria Station. She just looked at me. I didn't have to say a word.
"Are you alright, Gem?"
I daren't not speak for fear of crying. I shook my head and held back the tears. She whisked me off into the staff room at the back of the shop and I exploded into tears.

After that, I made sure someone, usually my sister, Judith, or Allan came with me to appointments. I needed support. I needed someone there to hear what was said. My memory was still bad and the effects of shock and panic stop me from listening properly and remembering.

You'd think that being in the medical profession, doctors would possess some kind of ability to deal with people and their feelings and reactions. But no – in my experience, not even basic counselling skills. If they are not able to do this as well as the other aspects of their job, then surely they should have someone on hand, a counsellor or something to help with this? Surely giving worrying information to a person who may have cancer and then just sending them off is not the best method?

Previously, I had told my consultant about this episode and was concerned that the neurologist, let's call him Dr C, would have been chastised for his malpractice and I was fearful of his response towards me and thought he might do something wrong on purpose. Judith told he wouldn't do that and of course he didn't. It was just my state of mind at the time. Getting back to the appointment, Dr C couldn't find the exact place to put in the needle. He was pressing and pushing on my scalp. I was worried he'd go to the wrong part of my head, miss it or worse, find the shunt and insert the needle at the wrong point and puncture it, then my shunt would not work and the fluid would go into the blood stream? I would die or I would have to have my shunt replaced?

Eventually, he found the correct point and withdrew some fluid but remarked, "There isn't quite enough fluid there." He had to leave the needle in my head a while longer, to see if the fluid in would flow any faster and then he could collect some more.

I was told that this procedure could provide the information they needed but if they didn't get enough fluid, I would need a biopsy. I visualised the fluid flowing in my brain going into the needle. I was willing it to flow – gush, anything not to have a biopsy.

He returned twenty minutes or so later, he thought he may have enough fluid but he wasn't sure. He told me he would send it off to be examined. At least he had some hope, I thought. But he had to send it off. **Send it off!** I wanted to know immediately. That meant more waiting.

It was nearly Christmas now. I went for a stay at my sister's and awaited news of my fate there. I tried to have a relaxing bath, lots of warm water, heaps of bubbles and soft fluffy towels. I emerged from the bath tub and sat on the bed with Judith. "Gem," she said. "I wasn't going to tell you, but the doctor just phoned while you were in the bath. He said he'd call back later." My mind and emotions were in turmoil. I was having the most agonizing time. Call back later! Sure! When? Right now, tomorrow, next week, who knows? Meanwhile, I have to wait, knowing he knows my fate and I don't! Oh God, I thought I'd stopped all this shaking business.

It was an hour maybe more when he called again, but it felt like forever. He said he was just sorting his desk out before the Christmas holiday and wanted to get everything cleared-up. There was not enough fluid and so I had to have a biopsy. They would contact me soon. As I write, I am still flabbergasted at this. Two days before Christmas Day. He didn't say, "Come in now, it's an emergency." No. He just said he'd contact me later in the New Year.

I didn't see the need for him to tell me this news just before Christmas, just because he wanted to clear his desk. He could have done this a few days or weeks later couldn't he? But as long as I helped him out by clearing his desk, that's OK.

"I'll bloody clear his desk!" I fumed. I was so angry with him and so scared.

I began to shake again.

Apart from Mum and Dad, I decided to wait until after Christmas Day to tell anyone else about this news. Why should everybody else's Christmas be ruined as well. This actually was a good idea, as not talking about it even just for one or two days and forgetting about it momentarily - well almost - made my day all the better.

I heard nothing for a number of weeks.

When eventually he did call, the doctor informed me he was going on holiday.

"That's nice," I thought. "I'd like to go on holiday too but I'm waiting for a biopsy." But I supposed that even he needed a holiday. He assured me that his colleague would do the biopsy instead, or, if I liked, I could wait for him to return. It was an easy decision. I didn't want to have to wait for him to return from holiday and for my tumour to have grown even more, causing goodness knows what damage to my brain.

I was booked to go in a few weeks later. At first, they couldn't give an exact date. I was to telephone each day to see if they had a bed spare. Didn't they realise how urgent this was for me? Did I really have to collapse, be ill enough to go to Accident and Emergency to get a bed? What were they waiting for? They told me I definitely needed a biopsy now.

I packed my bag in advance, ready to go in. I felt like a pregnant woman waiting for her waters to break.

Eventually, the day came for me to go in but I'd been told I should phone in the morning, just in case something happened. I did.
"No bed. The person in it at the moment is not ready to be released," I was informed. And, of course, I didn't want people to be thrown out because of me.
I phoned the next morning.
"Sorry, no bed."
And so it went on.
I demanded to speak to the neurosurgeon who was to perform the biopsy and I was cut off.
I rang back. Engaged.

It was enough to test anyone's patience. I thumped the kitchen table where I was sitting. I was angry, so frustrated and scared.

Allan, who was with me while I was making these calls, exploded. He made it clear that he really could be doing without a stroppy girlfriend right now.
"Fine!" I walked out of the room, slammed the door and went down to my room in the basement, and cried. Of course, he followed and comforted me. I guess he was under a lot of stress too, not just about me but because he was in the midst of retaking his accountancy exams. I was so consumed about myself I'd totally forgotten or appreciated that.

It was the end of January when eventually I got a bed in the hospital. They weren't sure of the date of the operation but they advised me to come into hospital and take the bed because "possession is nine tenths of the law. They can't turf you out if you are there." So I went along and awaited my operation.

How dull, depressing and lonely hospitals can be.

I was in a room of my own; good in one sense, a bit of privacy, but to me it felt very isolating. I took a walk around the adjacent wards. It looked scary. Room after room I could see there were very ill patients: bald-headed, with scars on their scalps. They looked totally out of it, all dressed in the white gowns stamped with the hospital logo. All you could hear were mad sounding moans and groans. It was incredibly grim. I wondered if I was in the right place.

So I was to sit and await my future with nothing better to think about but my operation, my tumour and my life, all day.
My cousin, Elaine, lived nearby and visited when she could and, of course, Allan did too. He didn't work anywhere near but still visited. He brought me travel brochures and promised to take me to Italy. "When it's all over, we'll go to the lakes. Here, have a browse."

My flatmate, Kate, brought over my TV in her car. I needed one to take my mind off it all especially as friends were finding it difficult to visit, as this hospital wasn't on a Tube line and the other side of London for them. Unfortunately, we couldn't get a TV reception so there was nothing else for me to do. I was left bored and terrified in anticipation of the date of my surgery. I don't remember how long I was there, maybe a week or two but do remember leaving the hospital one evening so I could go and visit my cousin Elaine. I had permission from the nurses but I did feel like a naughty teenager going out without telling your parents.

The neurosurgeon doing my operation came to see me. It winds me up just to think of him even after all these years. He was also so patronising: he had come to my bedside in the hospital. He was talking to a gaggle of minions who were running around after him. I hope they haven't learnt his appalling bedside manner.

He talked to them about me, as if I was not there, as if I was an object. Eventually, he asked, "Do you have any questions about your biopsy?"

I knew I was to have a small hole drilled into my scalp, about the size of a five pence piece (the old kind) and a small part of the tumour would be removed and examined.

I asked him how compos-mentis I would be after my operation, as Allan had said he would take time off work to be with me. I asked this because I thought he was the only person who I knew could come and visit and thought it wouldn't be worth his while taking this day off if I was going to be knocked out all day by the anaesthetic. He could take the next day off or another day when

I was awake. I didn't want to be too much of a burden to him. After all, I wasn't married to him or anything and I wasn't too sure how his work would be about taking time off just for a girlfriend.

The neurosurgeon replied that he really didn't know and told me to ask some 'sensible questions' rather than bothering about whether my boyfriend could be there or not. I felt like a pathetic girly but I needed to know. No one else as far as I knew was going to be there after my operation.

He left me furiously mad. He had been so condescending. I didn't tear him off a strip there and then, although I felt like doing that more than anything. The only reason I didn't was I kept thinking this was the man who was going to be cutting my head open and going into my brain. I didn't want him to be angry with me for fear of what he could do to me. I could already tell that he was already pissed off with me.

He'd warned me that there were risks if any slight errors were made any blood clotting from this biopsy and I'd be dead. He explained that this was unlikely and there was only a small chance of this happening. That really didn't help as the fact that it could happen and was a real possibility filled me with fear. I was in a state of terror. What if he **did** make a mistake? I was putting my life into his hands.

The date and time were set. I was to go into surgery at 8.00 am. I was more than ready for this. I just wanted it over and done with.
Allan was to travel over to see me very early.

I'd had my pre operation sedative and it was 7.30 am. No one came to collect me! I was to be there at 8.00 am sharp. If I wasn't on time they wouldn't be able to do the procedure today because the operation was to take place in the hospital across the road in The Maudsley and they could only use their premises for a certain period.
Allan had been, hugged and kissed and had gone off to wait a few hours. I was on my own.
"Shouldn't I be going now?" I called to a nurse.
"Oh no, it's a bit later. The ambulance man will be here soon to take you over."
This went on for a while longer.

My sister Nicola telephoned me from South Africa before I was wheeled down to theatre. It was her birthday and I thought it should have been me phoning her really. "Place yourself in Jesus' hands." She told me that and me that she and all her friends in South Africa would be praying for me all the while I was being operated on. I don't share her religious beliefs and she's a real evangelical Christian but somehow it did help. I thought what would be would be, and it did have a calming effect but whether it was Jesus or the pre- operation sedative working, I couldn't tell.

Again a phone rang somewhere nearby and it was an irate call from the neurosurgeon asking "Where the hell was Gemma?" as he needed to start now or he would miss the slot allocated for him to be in the theatre. He could not go over the time limit. I was going into a frenzy again. If my biopsy were to be delayed again I would go berserk. I would have missed my operation because some nurse had got the times mixed up! About half an hour later they collected me.

Relieved yet terrified, they strapped me to a stretcher and took me down to the waiting area where the ambulance man would take me across the road to the hospital.

I arrived in the waiting area ready to be wheeled into an ambulance. I waited for what felt like an interminable period. So I unstrapped myself from the stretcher, so I could at least sit up. I called over to the receptionist, "Excuse me, when am I going to be transported, my operation was due 10 minutes ago!"

"You'll have to wait your turn," she said.

She was being so bloody 'red tape'. I needed to be there. She didn't understand my emergency, my desperation. It felt like just one incompetency after another. I was about to explode with fury.

After thirty minutes of quietly fuming I was taken over to the hospital. I really needed to go to the toilet (I only tell you this now as it's important later) but I didn't dare tell them in case this delayed them even further and I'd miss the operation.

They wheeled me in, running down the corridors. We arrived at the theatre and voices were saying, "Sorry the surgeon's gone. He's not here. Where the hell have you been? He's been waiting for you for ages."

"He called your ward. Where were you? He's gone over to your ward to try and find you."

"I'm not sure we can do the operation now. It's too late."

That was it. I exploded. "I don't fucking believe this. Too bloody late? I've been fucking waiting for the fucking operation for fucking ages!" I screamed. "**I'm** too late, it's nothing to do with me. I tried to flipping well get them to take me down at the correct time but they wouldn't. I could have damn well walked across the sodding road to the flaming theatre quicker," I yelled. I really didn't want to be in such a fury just before a big operation like this.

Then someone called out, "It's OK. Go ahead. He's coming back. Quick, give her the anaesthetic."

Sometime later, I could feel myself coming round, then going back to sleep, coming round and going back to sleep. I had been wheeled to the end of a corridor beside a ward. I remember being given oxygen and feeling very nauseous and hurling up green bile.

I still needed to go to the toilet. It was desperate. They got a pan. I had to sit on it. There is no way I could sit on a pan, let alone sit up after brain surgery. I couldn't go, desperate or not. It was as if something inside me was holding on and saying, "No, I will not." Even though I was telling myself to, "just go".

I was left there alone and Allan was sitting nearby. How I wanted to cuddle him, speak to him, but I could hardly talk, my throat was all sore and I was feeling so sick and struggling to breathe. There were monitors hooked up all around me. They started to bleep. I don't remember too much but Allan told me he went into a panic, ran out of the room to get someone to help, angry at how could they just leave me unattended? He was scared I was going to die.

Nothing too serious happened but I was wheeled to a 'High Dependency Ward' to be kept under observation for 24 hours a day. From my bed, I could see Allan waiting in the corridor for me. He was there all day, just sitting there, just in case, just to be there. It was good to know he was around.

Mum and Dad appeared some time later. They squeezed my hand and had tears in their eyes. I was so pleased to see them as they had said they couldn't come. A day later or so, I still needed the loo. I tried again and was successful. I quietly mentioned it to a nurse. Well, that was it. The news spread round the ward like wild fire.
"She's done a stool, she's done a stool!" was the message from one nurse to another nurse to the doctors.
"Right. You're OK. You can go into an ordinary ward now." I was slightly embarrassed that everyone knew of my activity but also quite pleased. It must be the way you'd feel after having done the same thing in a potty for the first time, aged 2. However, I

wasn't going to tell them that it was the poo I'd needed before my operation and so it wasn't actually my digestive system working properly after the operation.

It was only a day later and they said I could go home. I was overjoyed. Mum and Dad drove me to their home to convalesce. I was informed that I would hear my biopsy results shortly. I knew that normally this happened pretty quickly, within days, or even hours. So I was told I'd know all, very soon.

That was not the case with me. After calling frequently, I was informed that the next available out-patient appointment would be in about two and a half weeks. This was not the immediate reply I'd hoped for and wasn't what other people had told me about their speedy responses.

As you see from the medical notes in my discharge summary, they diagnosed a low grade Pineocytoma.

What is a Pineocytoma and what can it do?
A Pineocytoma is a rare benign tumour. It is located in the centre of the brain between to hemispheres of the brain. See http://www.nervous-system-diseases.com/pineocytoma.html

Looking at this site years later it is alarming to me to see the possible symptoms of a pineocytoma. In short, it explains that it sits near where cerebrospinal fluid flows. This is fluid that everybody has flowing in their head. Its primary function is to cushion the brain within the skull and serve as a shock absorber for the central nervous system. It also circulates nutrients and chemicals filtered from the blood and removes waste products from the brain.

So my tumour, a pineocytoma - if it enlarges - can compress the aqueduct and block the normal flow of cerebrospinal fluid. This can lead to a condition known as hydrocephalus which is exactly what I had had two years before. This can cause enlargement of the ventricles and so increase pressure in the head. This can lead to symptoms such as headache, nausea, vomiting and finally neurological deterioration as it becomes more severe, again, the symptoms I had!!

I find this confusing as I was told that the operation I had for the hydrocephalus in July 1992 was not caused by a tumour. Had they missed something back then?

I am so glad that this consultant neurologist had been able to see what was going on, even if it was three years later. Part of me is mad about this and feels that it was malpractice. Surely, they could have done something sooner before I become so ill? Whatever they planned to give me if the lesion had been larger could have been done sooner rather than later? If it was going to help the larger lesions why wouldn't it help the small ones?

However, I had been told there was nothing they could do for me until they got larger. Nevertheless, even if they had seen the lesions/masses earlier they were not going to do anything at this point, apart from monitor.

Their findings had also shown that they had not found any malignant cells. When I was told about this, which was sometime much later, I had thought this was a really good sign, until it was explained to me more clearly. It didn't make too much difference if there were benign or malignant as they were in the centre of my head and this would damage my brain.

Chapter 3 – Treatment

After the consultant radiologist viewed my scans, they found evidence of a slow progression of a pineocytoma to the pituitary region in my brain. Radiotherapy was recommended.

I'd been warned how debilitating radiology could be by my sister-in-law Alice. Her mother had had radiology and she told me that she was exhausted by it and couldn't even get up to make herself a cup of tea. She had urged me to get treatment in Birmingham, where much of my family lived. I know it was said with the best of intentions as it meant my family would be able to look after me and care for me. But I didn't want to go to Birmingham as my friends and boyfriend lived in London and anyway, I hoped that I might not be so affected by the radiology. The nurses and radiologists didn't tell me there'd be a big problem.

My brother, Laurie, I think to alleviate my anxiety, had told me of one of his employees who had radiology and was able to return to work the same day. "Because that's the kind of girl she is," he said. He didn't understand. I wouldn't be returning back to work. I couldn't even make my way to the corner shop! Anyway, I'd been told that the radiology would destroy my tumour and that St Bart's was the best hospital. I was sure I'd be just fine.

First, I was to be fitted for a mask and be measured up so the radiographers would be able to direct the radium to my head. It was explained to me that radiology was aimed at killing my tumour cells. I wondered how could it kill some cells and not others? To get to the tumours, it would have to go through the rest of my brain. My tumours were in the middle of my head. Wouldn't it damage other parts of my brain too? I didn't understand but I trusted the doctors implicitly. A member of the consultant's team explained it a little more to me. For the first time in my experience, the staff were very supportive and answered my questions, concerns and worries.

Before I gave my consent, they took me aside and explained how it might affect me. They warned me that I might get tired but said that I ought to be able to cope because I was not going to have a lot of treatment. My scalp, where the radiology would be focused, might become red and itchy and feel like it had been burnt and I was not to scratch it or to wash my hair or brush it through the treatment period. My hair might fall out. However, it usually grows back but sometimes it takes a while. Sometimes it grows back a different colour, sometimes curly when it was straight or straight when it was curly and, as I later found out, sometimes it doesn't grow back at all.

Ok, I might lose my hair, but I felt sure it would grow back and this would be a minor upset and not something to concern myself with since my choices seemed clear cut. What did I care? Keep my hair and not have the treatment and die of a tumour and keep my hair. There was no contest, no decision to be made. As far as I was concerned, my doctor was the person who was going to get me better.

I gave my consent and signed the form.

MASK FITTING

The next thing to do was to prepare for my radiation treatment and have a mask made. This was to be made to measure to ensure my head would be held in exactly the same position every time I had my treatment.

To make a mask, the technician made a plaster cast of my face. This meant the whole of my face and neck was covered completely with strips of wet bandages and covered with plaster, with only a small mouth and nose holes to breathe through. I had never felt claustrophobic before but I sure did then. I had already felt that fear when in the MRI machines but this was on an entirely different level. I had to lie very still for about 30 minutes and wait until the plaster set.

As I lay on the stretcher, I heard every pulse in my body. I felt totally enclosed, my senses cut off. It was like being in a coffin and knowing you're alive and not being able to move. I was told it could take a couple of weeks before I would have my treatment. I would need to wait for the mask to dry to have it double checked that it fitted. I was getting impatient. Now that that the decision had been made and I'd built myself up to the realisation that I was actually going to have radiology I wanted to get started and get it over and done with. There seemed to be so much preparation which was taking weeks to complete.

Around this time I'd been complaining of severe pains in my stomach area. I was worried that there was a problem with my shunt. I'd have to press really hard on the right hand side of my body to get any relief. Sometimes at night it would wake me up and I'd be flipping around like a fish out of water with the pain. Changing sides or turning over on to my back or stomach gave me no relief. My sister had concerns about this and wondered whether tumours had travelled down to that area as well.

My family alerted the neurosurgeon to this. Subsequently he arranged for me to have a barium meal to examine and then xray my gastrointestinal tract for any abnormalities. It was arranged as soon as possible which happened to be on the same day before my first radiology session.

RADIOTHERAPY SESSIONS

The day of my planned treatment finally arrived. I had been told not to eat 12 hours before my barium meal. My stomach must be empty. Once there, I had to drink a number of pints of blackcurrant flavoured water with another ingredient in it which would show up on their scanner and reveal any lumps or masses that shouldn't be there. The drink tasted OK, but there was so much of it and I was not to go to the toilet before being scanned as if anything was there, it wouldn't show up. So I crossed my legs and drank, determined not to go, as I didn't want to have to go through all this procedure again. I had my scan and waited for the results and went to the radiology department.

I had been told my doctor was very prompt with his appointments and I was to make sure I was on time or else I would miss my slot and I really didn't want that to happen! I was seated in a wheelchair and wheeled to the lift taking me to the basement where I was to be treated. I was allowed to bring in some music for them to play while I had my treatment, in the hope that it would take my mind off things. As I'd been told, I made sure I was not wearing anything metal, no belt buckle, no under-wire bra and no jewellery. I lay on the table, on my stomach; face fastened into the moulded plastic suffocating mask and let the huge machine zap my head.

I was to be in the room on my own. No one else, not even the nurses, could enter the room during this procedure.

After my treatment, I went back to my house in a taxi with my friend, Anna. I felt so nauseous as the taxi drove me home. My stomach churned as we speeded over another sleeping policeman. I yelled at the driver to stop. I was going to be sick. I flung the taxi door open as it came to a halt - I couldn't get out quick enough. It stopped by a Victorian terraced house with three floors, so there was a basement room below the street level. My vomit flew over their iron bars, down to their

basement floor. I just hoped the owners weren't looking out of the window at that moment. How vile for them!
I felt so embarrassed, like some drunk, throwing up out of a taxi. Anna explained to the driver that I'd just had radiotherapy and mopped up the sick in the back of the car. My poor friend. I apologised profusely.

Eventually, we arrived back home. I was freezing. I sat on the sofa. I was shaking all over. I was so cold. Anna went to make some lunch. I was so hungry after having starved myself for the barium meal. I curled up on the lounge sofa, well it wasn't really a sofa, just one of my house mate's bed mattress we used as a sofa and covered myself with duvets and blankets with a bucket at my side, just in case.

A frozen, microwave meal-for-one was heated and brought into the lounge. I was feeling OK 'till the smell of the food hit my nostrils. I heaved and was sick again. I was taken down to my bedroom.

I felt so ill and so sorry for myself. I got into bed with a hot water bottle and again, covering myself with two duvets, a blanket and the bucket beside me. I couldn't stop shaking. A short while later in the afternoon, Allan appeared. I was pleasantly surprised. It was the middle of the day. He should have been at work. It turned out that my house mate, Kate, had called him and explained how I was. He'd come over immediately.

From then on, Allan came over most evenings. I'd be sleeping mostly and he'd be upstairs with his laptop catching-up with work he had missed. I was just happy to have him around, just in case something happened.

Kate had also called the radiology department. I could go into hospital if I wanted, or take one of the tablets they had given me to hold on to, just in case I got sick. So I thought I'd try that first and talk to them the following day when I was to have radiology again.

The tablets did seem to help. I didn't seem as nauseous. I went in the next day for my appointment. The radiologist was perplexed at me being violently ill so soon and thought it was a reaction from the barium meal I'd had that day. He had spoken to the relevant department and they had said no way was it the barium meal, it was the radiology. Either way, I did not want to continue with this kind of reaction. I'd only had one treatment and I was to have a daily dose for four weeks with the weekends and the odd day off in between.

I returned home after another treatment. Mum phoned. She said that her friend, Nicky, had had cancer and she had told her that there were some really strong tablets to take if you got bad. They would only give them when you were really, really ill. I was not to worry because there were even stronger tablets available should I need them.

She told me they were called "Zofran." They don't give them out that often, only as a last resort. They were really expensive, £10 a pill.

"Those are the ones I've been given!"

Mum was silent.

Each day I went with one friend or another by taxi to have my treatment. I'd be greeted by the chirpy receptionists, who always remembered your first name and always asked how you felt. I was amazed how they always recognised me. I could never remember which one was called what. I liked their familiarity and jovial manner. It was a nice change. They were so positive, making jokes and telling patients how great they looked in their new hat or wig or what a beautiful shaped head they had, when it was red and scaly with patches of hair. Sometimes my head would become so itchy I'd have to sit on my hands to stop myself from scratching it.

After a number of sessions, I was reviewed and the consultant radiotherapist told me the treatment had not done as well as expected. I was to have, what he called some boosters. The radiology would be directed directly on my tumours and not just on the whole of my head this time. With the threat of my hair falling out I asked the him if he would avoid the treatment on my eyebrow area. I just couldn't cope them falling out as well as my hair, should that happen.

A new appointment was made. I was to go to the treatment room for them to mark with a pen on the mask exactly where the treatment would be aimed at on my head. It was essential to get it correct to the millimetre, so there would not to damage any other part of my brain. Again, I lay on the table, face fastened into the moulded mask. I was bolted down with screws and the radiologists looked at the scan of my brain and marked, very accurately and very carefully on the mask exactly where the rays were to be directed. I was not to move an inch or their calculations would be incorrect. There was a window through which I could see the radiologists controlling computers to position the machinery but once bolted down I could only stare at the floor through the eyeholes in my mask. I felt so scared, so terrified. What if I moved? What if I sneezed, coughed? I was shaking but I think it was only internally. "Would that affect where they marked"?

I was then to return for another appointment for my new radiotherapy sessions. Before treatment began the consultant leapt into the room and ordered everything to come to an immediate halt. He looked alarmed and said I need to be marked up again. They had seen something else. I was to go and have this checked and have another MRI scan before he could proceed. My mind was again in turmoil. I'd been told the barium meal had not shown up anything abnormal.
"Oh God, what if there's another tumour, another wait before they would treat me and get rid of this damn thing."
I was in despair.

The MRI scan indeed revealed that it had spread. I felt as if it was taking over my body. Why hadn't they treating me sooner? Why had they waited so long? So long that it had now spread! Had it been there last time I had a scan and all their procrastination left me riddled with tumours? I was so angry. Why had they waited until this stage? Why didn't they treat it when it was smaller and only in one place?

I felt as if I had no control over them or my body.

They discovered it had spread to my spine. I was measured up again so that the radiology would be directed at my brain and my spine. They made ink marks on my skin on my back where they would direct the radiation, down my spine which I was told were not to be washed off. I felt like a butcher's carcass. I was not to have a bath until my treatment was complete or the carefully crossed points on my back would come off in the water and they would have to mark me up again.

I have always made sure I was clean and I bathe and or shower at least once a day. Now I prefer to have two baths a day really, as it was the only way I could warm myself up. I was always 'cold to the bone' as they say and could feel every bone in my body. In bed, I'd have walking socks on, a thermal vest, pyjamas, two duvets and a blanket and a hot water bottle. Not having a bath was quite a thing for me but of course I complied and went without my bathing. I wanted to avoid any more delays.

I was panicking that the radiographer's crosses would rub off and, true to form, in the following few nights the markings almost faded away. I worried it would delay my treatment. My housemate helped me out by going over them with a felt tip pen. "Be careful! Only mark exactly where they have marked," I had pleaded.

Towards the end of my treatment I was admitted to hospital with headaches, nausea, vomiting and dizziness. However, there did seem to be some beneficial benefits to all of this, I thought. My other housemate Jo came to visit. "You've lost so much weight Gemma. You've gone all skinny." A nurse had weighed me and confirmed this, telling me that I was at my optimum weight for my height. I'd been working on this for some time and now without even trying, without having missed any meals and without any exercise I had lost weight. I was delighted.

The nutritionist visited and praised me for my weight, but as it continued to fall, she asked me one day if I had ever thought of eating an extra pudding with my dinner?

I called my friends and my regular visitors, to tell them my good news. I had been told to have an extra pudding with my meal.

Friends were always wanting to know what to bring me on their visits, so I was going to make it easy for them. News got around and an influx of delicious assortment of creamy, chocolaty and fruity puddings were bought in at each visit. Deirdre was particularly good at this, not knowing whether I'd prefer a Marks & Spencer creamy lemon mousse, or a raspberry trifle or a chocolate fudge cake, she would bring in a selection. Well, what could I do but try each of them out? Of course, there was no need for deliberation, all were delicious.

Dina, another house mate came on a regular basis. She worked close by and in her lunch hour would push me in a wheelchair down to the lift and outside to the hospital courtyard. It felt great to be outside, not to be stuck in the same surroundings and stuffy air and to have sunshine on my face. Dina screeched as the pigeons flapped around us, as she ate her lunch. After a chat and a brief encounter with the outside world, she'd would push me back to my bed and return to work.

WIGS

During my treatment I had asked the radiologist if I could have a wig sorted out for me in advance just in case my hair fell out. I didn't want to wait till it fell out and then have to wait to get one made as I didn't want to go around with a balding, red scalp.

I was advised to go to the Surgical Appliance Department. Judith came with me. We made our way over the hospital courtyard into a building that seemed to lack activity. It was quiet and a bit spooky. We went up in the old chugging lift, along a silent corridor to a door with a paper note stuck on it "Surgical Appliance Unit." We knocked and entered.

All around were dismembered plastic bits of bodies. A leg hanging over there, a forearm on the desk and a foot on the shelf. In the middle of this was an elderly woman at her desk surrounded by a flurry of paper work.
"I'd like to be fitted for a wig."
I wanted a real hair wig, not one of those nylon wigs that looks like a wig, the kind I'd been given when I had hydrocephalus. I knew that patients were only allowed to have real hair wigs if

they were going to be bald for years and can cost lots of money, hundreds of pounds or more.

"You can't have real hair. You can only have one if you have long term alopecia and you're completely bald. What's wrong with you?" she said very abruptly.

I know I have a fantastic ability to look extremely well when I'm really ill but I just wanted a wig. I didn't want to have to justify to her why I needed one.

I felt embarrassed to have to go and ask for a wig. It was awful to know that your hair might fall out. Already a few strands had. It felt intrusive of her to be asked these questions.

I'd told her that I'd been advised to see her by the neurosurgeon. What more did she need? I was angry and upset with her. It was her job to find a wig not to decide whether I needed one. Surely that was none of her business. She sat me down and tried to convince me that real hair was not as good. A patient had come to see her a while back, she told us, and she had always wanted long blonde curly hair, so insisted on having a real hair wig. It had looked dreadful on her, I was told. It wasn't her style or colour and she had wished she had gone for the nylon one.

"Here," she said, "Have a look at this magazine and pick one out and you can try it on."

I was irritated. I didn't want one of these wigs but I thought I'd give it a go while I was here. I pointed to a couple. "Samantha," she called to her assistant. "Get a 'Jackie' and a 'Veronica' out, would you?"

All the wigs had names.

At my next appointment with them, they said that the radiologist had written a letter for the Surgical Appliance Department to allow me to have a real hair wig. I was told that I had been granted this as I was a young woman and had gone through a lot. I was very pleased. "Some well-deserved sympathy at last," I thought. In retrospect, I think maybe he thought I wouldn't get my hair back as he was planning on more treatment.

Meanwhile, Judith and I had gone to a wig maker, recommended in a B.A.C.U.P. charity booklet on cancer. The woman working there was really helpful. She explained that actually nylon wigs are easier to care for. A real hair wig reacts like real hair and so may frizz up in damp weather and will need to be washed more frequently. Whereas nylon wigs are more likely to behave and stay in the desired style regardless of the weather. Anyway, she convinced me.

Previously, Judith and I had scanned London department stores for other wig possibilities. They were either short grey curly ones for old ladies or florescent pink or blue ones for teenage fancy dress parties. At this time there was a definite gap in the market for young adults like me.

I wanted a wig that resembled my natural hair colour and the style I'd had previously. I'd had my hair cut that way because that's what I liked. I didn't want different colour or style. I wanted it to remain the same as it was. After searching all the likely stores we knew of that might sell wigs, we tried Harrods. They had a better selection and I wanted to try some on. I was taken into a small side room, as is the protocol for those who want to try on wigs. It gives you some privacy.
At this point I wasn't balding, just really greasy as I'd been told not to wash it during the treatment.

As the assistant looked in the store room for my chosen wig, she handed me a piece of paper. It read "A £6 charge will be made to try on wigs."

I was outraged, and told Judith, "She can forget it and keep her wigs." They were already asking around £100 for a wig and wanted me to pay to try one on! What is this, a punishment for being ill and for having to have radiology treatment? The assistant returned and having heard some of our conversation said that she realised that I was a genuine case and not just messing about, as kids had done in the past and retracted the extra expense.

I put the wig on. It was the first, after many that instantly looked halfway normal on me. In fact, it looked great. I went home, now in possession of a new wig, to keep, just in case.

Mouthwash

With my treatment I was also advised to use a mouthwash before and after every meal. The radiology was likely to affect my gums and lead to problems with my teeth. A mouth wash was essential I had been told. So, after each meal I religiously gargled.

I love my food and I always have three meals a day.

There wasn't a lot left for me to do. So something delicious for lunch was something to look forward to.

This wash tasted vile. It made the taste of the food horrible and didn't allow me to savour any of it as I'd have to rush upstairs to rinse straight after eating. The smell of it almost made me gag. It completely ruined the best part of my day. My pleasure from food went. Another thing that I'd felt that had been taken from me.

At the end of the radiotherapy sessions which I had from the 22nd April to 7th June 1996, I was told that it hadn't been as successful as they'd hoped.
"There's been no change."
My heart sank. All my hopeful anticipation dissolves and transforms into despair.

The consultant flicks through my notes. "Oh, what's this? I hadn't noticed this. The report says the tumours in your spine have diminished. So that's good news Gemma."
Hope and relief flooded back.

"However, your improvement is not enough to continue with the radiology. I think we should plough ahead and proceed with some chemo sessions"

"So, was this good news?" I thought.

I was confused. The tumours in my spine had gone and I'd been told it was not a good enough result so why wouldn't he continue with what was working? Nevertheless, I trusted him and was sort of pleased, perhaps more relieved that there was another treatment to continue the good work. But there was this nagging doubt. Radiology to chemotherapy didn't sound too much of a progression. Was I flinging myself from one disaster to another?

Before my chemo treatment I had a PET scan. PET stands for positron emission tomography. It can show how body tissues are working, as well as what they look like. It can help to diagnose and stage a cancer. This helps your doctor decide which treatment you need and whether your treatment is working.

You can see from my medical notes they had surmised that it says that my vision is worse and that I have "enhancing mass tissue" and "the tumour is viable in the pineal area" that is, that the tumour had got worse in the pineal gland but he didn't mention that bit to me. He wants to give me chemotherapy to finish the treatment course as the letter says "It will be the same treatment they use for pineoblastoma because her pineocytoma has declared itself as an aggressive metastasising tumour."

Pineocytoma a benign, slowly growing tumour of the pineal gland Pineoblastoma is a cancerous (malignant) tumour that develops in the pineal gland. Metastases the spreading of cancer from one part the body to another.

Chemotherapy

A plastic bag of chemo is hanging on a pole next to my bed. There is a tube from it going into my arm. It looks a bit like a drip does. The pole is on some wheels, so this means I can get up and take myself round the ward or to the toilet I am told.
Walking, stick in one hand, pole on wheels in the other is quite a skill. Once I reach the bathroom cubical I aim my rear towards the toilet seat, fearful about accidentally pulling out the needle in my arm that feeds in the chemo drugs. "At least I'm not on a catheter at the moment," I thought.

Along with this treatment, I was taking some homoeopathic remedies which were aimed at helping the side-effects people sometimes get from having chemotherapy. I'll explain about that in the next chapter.

Allan visited and said he had plans to go on a motor bike tour with a friend around France. Something he'd always wanted to do. It was just for a month.

"I'll send a postcard to you every day, Gem, and I'll call you. I'll come right back, straight away if you get any worse. Promise me you will tell if anything happens."

I watched him leave the ward. I expected to feel devastated but I rationalised it out. He needed a well-earned break from all these goings on and it is a dream of his to travel the world on a motor bike.

I talked to Tonia, my sister. We decided that the positive side of this is that I'd get more visitors as friends and relatives would be more likely to visit if they thought no one else would.

Sure enough they did.

I waited for my next visitor. Of course, this was Anna, with my daily alternative lunch, salmon and dill sandwich, a fresh fruit yoghurt juice and of course, a yummy dessert. It was so much tastier than the food provided by the hospital.

I am just returning from the toilet, when a nurse approaches me.

"A man is waiting for you. He's very handsome," she says.

I thought, "Allan is away, so what man would be visiting?"

"He's got dark hair and is quite tall" she said.

"So has Allan has returned already. Maybe he is missing me too much and has come back for me"

I look round to the ward door. It's not Allan, but I am delight to see it's my brother, Laurie. He is tall and dark haired but I hadn't thought of him as handsome. I really hadn't thought about him in that way before but I suspect others might think so.

"Don't tell him I think he is handsome," the pink-cheeked nurse pleads.

It was nice to have time on my own with my brother, just one-to-one and not in a big family group. We chatted and he had to leave to drive back to his family in Birmingham. He promised to visit again.

The nurse rushes over to me after Laurie leaves. "Is that your boyfriend? He is rather dishy" I smile to myself and told her that he is my brother and married with two children.

Sue, Debbie, Kate, Elaine, cousin Geraldine and Auntie Vida visit, Judith visits, Sharon visits, and, of course, Mum and Anna visit me the most regularly, always with the Evening Mail crossword, food and/or chocolate and now bottles of water as I'd been to drink 5 litres a day.

NIGHT TIME

Nobody visited at night though. This is the time when I am alone with my fears. This is the time I cannot sleep. Not only is my mind active and busy worrying, so is my body. My body clock had switched. I was wide awake in the middle of the night and tranquil in the day and I could feel my body twitching and my legs had to move and stretch. I was wide-awake but I knew I needed to sleep, so I will be awake for my visitors the next day as sometimes they would visit when I was sleeping and so not to disturb me, leave a note to say they had been. I so wished they had woken me up.

I told myself to sleep but I couldn't help worrying about my tumours and about money and my hair loss and my fast depleting eyesight.

It was no good I had to get up, carefully mind, so not to wake the snoring patients but where would I walk to, what would I do? I am wide awake and had more energy in me than in the day.

The night nurse showed me a side room with a TV in. I switched from channel to channel. Two of the channels are not tuned in, the other two channels are of no interest, and - of course- there is no Sky TV, and anyway it is pointless as my eyes are not focusing well enough to see a picture anyway.
I returned to my bed. I lay there and wished the night away, waiting for morning when I finally drop off to sleep.
It was not long after that the auxiliary nurse would come to wake me to check my blood pressure. It's fine and off she goes to wake the next patient.

I wait for another two hours when I have breakfast. Then another two before my visitors arrive. Now I was exhausted and I tried and keep my eyes open.

In between sessions of my radio and chemo treatment I would sometimes go to Sue and Anna's flat, as it was near to the hospital and much quieter and peaceful than the hospital ward. Anna or Sue, like a hamster, would move all their belongings from one of their rooms to the other room and share so Mum and me could share a room. I had the futon whilst mum had the camp bed she'd brought from Bewdley, where she and Dad lived.

Of course, I was exhausted on arriving and have to go to sleep but there were a few days when I'd have a fit of energy and walk up Finchley Road with mum and have a spending spree. I remember on one occasion, I saw this long orange dress. I loved it. I'd never worn anything orange before and had only dressed in black for years. I even got some orange shoes to match. I'd been miserable for so long and had slimmed right down so what else would you do? Next, we bought a set of yellow dinner plates and bowls from Whittards as they were on sale. It cheered me up immensely. You see we must have been optimistic of my treatment and my future at that time to have bought a set of dinner plates. A bit of shopping therapy can go a long way.

The first cycle of chemo had revealed my condition had deteriorated, although my tumour was smaller and there was no evidence of new disease. I was admitted for a second cycle of chemo, which had been postponed for 4 weeks as there had been damage the bone marrow which was causing a low platelets count, and so I was given a reduced dose of chemo.

Regardless, the upshot of this was, as my medical notes say, "She continues to worsen."

Chapter 4 - Homoeopathy

You would think that you'd remember the gradual disintegration of yourself but I can't, but just to update you at about this time I'd put on 4 stone in 4 weeks as a result of the steroids that I'd been prescribed to try and help the tumours to shrink. Not only that but, because my body had grown at such a quick pace, the skin's elasticity couldn't keep up and so all over my body, my upper arms, my breasts, my hips and my thighs were streaked with bright purple from it's inability to stretch quickly enough. These weren't the small silver stretch mark like those you can get after pregnancy. Mine were red slashes and the size of Zebra markings.

On top of that, all my hair had fallen out in one weekend in between my radiotherapy sessions. There were there only the odd, very stubborn, strand or two left. I looked like a baby chick. At the same time, due to the testosterone in the steroids I had been told, I was growing hair in other places: on my shoulders, down my back; I had a small moustache - not your stereotypical middle-eastern male but still a very noticeable dark line. I was turning into a MAN? No, I think a MONSTER. My eyelids wouldn't open voluntarily. To see, I had to physically lift one lid with my finger. My eyesight was so bad at that time, I had flickering double-vision. It was so poor that I couldn't watch TV or read a book. I had a stick to walk with to help my balance. So I was fat, bald and stripy. I couldn't bear to look at myself.

One afternoon, sitting in the lounge at my mum's, the phone rang and it was Sharon, my sister-in-law. She told me that she'd spoken to a woman who said she "might be able to help me." She was a homoeopath whatever that was.

Sharon had taken her daughter to this homoeopath for help with her eczema. Whilst there, seeing that Sharon was upset about something, the homoeopath asked how she was and so she her all about me. So Sharon phoned to tell me about her.
I'd never heard of homoeopathy. Sharon said it was kind of like counselling. You talk things through and you get tablets.
Did I want to see her, I was asked.

Well, at that point, the radiology hadn't helped much and I seemed to be going from bad to worse. I certainly felt I could do with someone else to talk to, so I agreed. I had nothing to lose.

So it was arranged that Janice, my soon-to-be homoeopath, would travel from Birmingham to Worcester to see me. All I knew about her was that she used to be a French teacher. I remember thinking, "Oh no, a teacher." I hated learning French at school and now I was going to tell a former French teacher all about myself. I am afraid she got minus points for that, even before I met her.

I made a big effort to get dressed and go downstairs for my appointment. As my memory was so poor, I had asked Mum and Dad to sit with me so that they could listen in and I could check with them later.

Unconvinced as I was at that time, I remember that day vividly. In she walked. I couldn't detect any obvious signs of her having been a teacher. She came armed with many bags and books and a steel case. So I had my first consultation with a homoeopath. Mum gave her a photograph of how I used to look.
Years later, Janice told me that she wouldn't have known that the girl in the photos was me.

This photograph is me on holiday with Allan after a couple of years after my operation for hydrocephalus.

This is a photo of me and my sister at my worst.

There were a lot of questions about my health, about my family's health, my time-line –which is important, memorable moments in my life. I had made a time-line before in a counseling course. It was easier now than it was then, as I felt I'd not done much back then but this time I had a lot more to say.

Janice asked me lots of questions. It seemed to me to be taking ages and I was getting inpatient. As I said, I'd made a special effort to get dressed and come downstairs which was a huge task for me at this time. What with the consultation and having to wait for her to sort out the indicated remedies for me, I was getting tired and I told her to "hurry up".

She gave me a remedy and told me to take it straight away. I did and, after 2 maybe 3 seconds, I felt the urge to go to the toilet. I pulled my eyelid up, heaved myself up with my stick and made my way to the downstairs toilet.

A short time later, I returned.
All eyes were on me, my dad's, my mum's and Janice's.
"Well?" they said.
"What happened?"

It was a bit delicate to tell them what happened then, let alone for me to tell you, the unknown reader, what happened. You'll need some background. You see, I hadn't had a... how do you say it, a Number 2 - a big job - a shit - a poo - passed a stool - whatever, I hadn't had a bowel movement for weeks and weeks. I am not exaggerating here.

All the drugs that I had been given had constipation as a possible side-effect. The hospital had tried everything, apricot syrup, suppositories, enemas and I had eaten lots of dried fruits. No wonder I was so fat. I was full of shit and, basically, if I didn't die of cancer, I'd die of constipation.

Can you imagine, "What did your daughter die of?" "Constipation."

For me, I thought this event was a complete coincidence and I thought, if it was her doing, then homoeopathy is good for constipation, but I had cancer. I would need more proof than this.

Previously, before my appointment, my dad had darted down to the local library to get all the books he could on homoeopathy to investigate this unknown therapy to see what it was all about, finding out how it worked and its history. Also, I suspect, to see if it was anything to do with the devil or dark powers. My parents are strict Catholics.

What Dad found out was that it was a very old principle of healing going back hundreds of years, which was reinvestigated and developed by a German doctor in the 19th century. The German doctor, Samuel Hahnemann, had been disillusioned with the medication of his day such as blood-letting and application of leeches which had been common practice at this time.

Hahnemann had wanted to reduce the poisonous effects of large doses of toxic medicine in use at that time. For instance, mercury was uses for the treatment of syphilis. Even scientists today consider medicine of the 18th and 19th century as unscientific and even barbaric. He looked at diluting medicines and discovered if they then shaken vigorously -a process known as succussion, they became stronger in their effect, regardless of them being diluted and having less of the original substance in them. The dilution and succussion of the medicine is vital or else the remedy will not work.

He read that homoeopathic medicine is made-up of completely natural things from the plant, mineral and animal kingdom. For instance, a remedy made from a flower, the petals, leaves or stems may be used and would be finely chopped, ground and mixed with alcohol. This results in what is known as a mother tincture. One drop of this is then put into a test tube containing 9 drops of alcohol and succussed. From that tube a drop is placed into another test tube and succussed again. This process can be done several times, depending on how dilute you want the mix to be. When you get to the desired dilution a drop of the remedy is added to bottle of carrier pill made from sugar.

Currently, modern science says there is no physical trace of the original substance and yet homoeopaths, in certain disease states, may find a more dilute remedy to be the most successful. As my Dad read on he learnt that homoeopath is very holistic and prescribes remedies which are carefully considered to fit the patient's symptoms. There is not just one remedy for an aliment but many, depending on the individual's symptoms and medical history. So for example, a patient whose key symptoms are that they have a sudden high fever, where there is often an injured part that is throbbing, has dilated pupils, looked bright red and hot but their hands and feet were icy cold and has little thirst, a common remedy often used in acute situations would be belladonna. As you may know this is a flower with poisonous berries to be avoided but made up into a homoeopath potency it is one of the important fever and headaches remedies. So if you imagine if you did eat some of this flower you would be highly likely to get similar symptoms to that of the said patient, high fever, a red face and dilated pupils. In this way a main principle of homoeopathy is known as Like cures Like or The Law of Similars.

Another example of a remedy appropriate for someone with a fever but where the symptoms differ, a different remedy would be more appropriate. The belladonna would not work as the symptoms do not match for that individual. For example, if a person with a fever and was extremely anxious and restless and extremely thirsty but can only take small sips of cold water a key symptoms for a particular remedy called Arsenicum Album maybe more appropriate .

My dad was rather taken with all this, as it all seemed suddenly so obvious. "Of course, nature heals itself. God made everything we need on earth." He seemed to have made something that seemed so bizarre and unscientific into something very logical. Janice came to see me three times a week for up to 3 hours a time at first. It seemed intense to me especially as I was still so exhausted from my radiology treatment. I had told Janice that my oncologist had told me that I needed to go on to have chemotherapy.

Janice gave me remedies to take alongside the chemotherapy to help with any side-effects, such as nausea.

I was put me on a strict diet: no dairy, no sugar, no E numbers, no additives, no caffeinated tea or coffee, no alcohol, no cheese, no chocolate and no cups of tea.

"How would I be able to get up in the morning without a cup of tea"? I'd thought.

I was a bit sceptical, I knew tea has only a little bit of caffeine in it but surely it was not going to harm me to have a few cups now and then. But, no, I was only to have water, not even orange cordial because of the sugar and E numbers.

Chapter 5 - Bewdley – My Death Bed

I was lying in my bed. Every part of my body ached. I feel like I've been rolled over by a steamroller, you know the ones that flatten the tarmac when roads are made. I had been up all night as my legs were hurting me so much. I've never felt pain that bad before. I got up out of bed. My Mum and Dad hadn't heard me ring the bell that they'd left by the side of my bed to get their attention if needed. I used to love to ring that bell when I was a kid. I was always reprimanded and told to leave it alone. It made such a din so I'm not surprised. Now that I was allowed to ring it, no one could hear it, there room was too far away!

I called out to Mum, she didn't hear. I got up and went to my parents' bedroom.
"Mum, my legs are killing me." Tears were running down my face. "Get the doctor."
"You're not due another painkiller until the morning." Said replied.
Mum got up and told me to get back in bed and relax and she'd massage my legs for me.
It felt lovely. I wished she'd do it full time, all night.
I calmed down a bit and was left to return to sleep.

It was a while later. "Mum they're hurting again. Call the doctor, get an ambulance."

"There's nothing a doctor can do in the middle of the night. I can't wake the doctor up. There'll just be a receptionists' message saying to call in the morning if I call the surgery. Just try and relax."

I pleaded "Why won't you phone? I just need something to kill the pain. They can do something. They numb your body for operations don't they? So they can numb my legs."

I was in agony.

"Call an ambulance!"

They wouldn't. I was so incensed, "I'll call one myself!"

"Gem, don't. Wait 'till the morning and I'll ring the doctor first thing."

I was so angry, as the telephone number of the doctor was downstairs. I couldn't even flaming well get downstairs by myself at this point! It was so frustrating.

Of course, with a brain tumour, other parts of your body start to course you problems, as the tumour grows and can damages the brain nerves so messages from the brain can't be made anymore. That, coupled with the side effects of the drugs the doctors prescribed, I felt I didn't stand a chance. I did have one tablet I had was for neuralgia which obviously wasn't working for me and anyway a painkiller is a painkiller it doesn't actually heal anything, it just attempts to lessen the pain. I was miserable in my bed. The days were long. It got dark early and it rained most of the time. There was nothing to do. I still couldn't watch TV, I couldn't read, as my eyelids weren't working properly. I even had to get help to go to the toilet. Mum bathed me. I was just waiting to die. I was dreading the process of it all. I was getting worse and worse. I felt like a vegetable.

I said to Allan and to Mum that if I was put on a life machine, they were to switch it off. I'd recently heard a couple of stories that had hit the newspapers about people who'd gone into comas and come round up to nine years later. I didn't want to do that. That's surviving, not living.

I'd just spoken to Judith on the phone. She put it as delicately as she could. "It's a really good idea to make a will. Syd and I have done this for ourselves. It doesn't mean you're going to die but it just makes it easier for those left behind if you do suddenly die." A while later I set about making my will.
I didn't have anything to give away. Not of any value anyway. I did have some pieces of jewellery Kate made me, which were

frequently admired. I'd give my rings to Tonia, my earrings to Sue and Anna but what would I give Allan? What could I possibly give to Allan? I'd give him my necklaces that I wore most days, as a keep sake, but what about my other brothers and sisters I can't give one sister or brother something and nothing to another. What could I give?

I'd give my oil painting of some sunflowers, that my Grandmother had painted, to my Mum, but what to give to Dad. This making a will thing was making me too anxious. I didn't want to leave anyone out or to seemingly show more affection to one more than another.

I wrote my will out as clearly as I could. When Mum next came up to see me I told her where I'd put it just in case. We went through it together to make sure she could read it all. Mums eyes filled with water as she clutched my hand.

Of course I had suicide thoughts. I didn't want to be in the process of dying for years. If I was to die, I wanted to die now, not have to go through days or years of pain. I might as well end it now rather than go through all of that.

I thought about it quite a lot. How could I do it? It would have to be quick. I couldn't stab myself and bleed to death. I didn't want to have to slit my wrists or hang myself. Too gruesome, too gory and anyway I'm too much of a coward to inflict pain on myself.

I'd hoped to speak to Tonia. She knew doctors, as she worked in the National Health. Maybe she could get me something. I could overdose on something strong as I didn't want to wake up the next day, stomach pumped, in hospital. I would have to consult with her. Reluctantly she told me she could not do this for me.

I spoke to Judith on the phone about it. Maybe I'll jump off a bridge and fall to my death I told her.
"Oh Gem don't think that. Anyway, that would be awful for the drivers. What if you're not successful? You'll end up maimed as well as having cancer."
"Umm, that would just be my luck." I thought. "I'll have to think of something else." Now I really know what those people who have been denied Euthanasia feel like.

I had an overbearing feeling that this just wasn't fair as I haven't done anything I really wanted to do in life and as the youngest in my family it's not right that I die first. Surely it's the other way round. "I'm supposed to be the last to go aren't I"? This is not the order nature intended.

When I told Mum some of what I'd been thinking. I felt a bit reticent about it because she'd always been a bit scathing about people who commit suicide, saying "They are so selfish. What about the ones they leave behind?" It's a sin to take your own life in Catholicism.

I didn't care. What is the point of me suffering? As far as was I'm concerned at this point, you die, you rot in the ground and make good humus to fertilize the soil and that's it. No more, no less. Heaven and hell are here in life and right now I was in hell.

October 1996

It was October and the day I was to go back into hospital to get some results. The hospital bed where I had been a week before had been saved for me as I'd been given the option of remaining on the ward or returning home. I think it was just because there was no point me being there until I got the results? My mother had since told me she was perplexed and a little confused and concerned at this news. Wondering why would they leave an empty bed for me?

The following week, Allan, my Mum, Anna and Judith all came with me. We wait and wait for the oncologist to appear with my recent results. Trying to be mindful that, that's the way it is. However we were all impatient and full of plastic cups of tea and had long completed the newspaper crossword.

Finally, he arrived. I was lying on my bed. The curtains were drawn around me, Mum and Judith beside me. Allan pushed the curtain aside and stepped in.
"Are you family?" asked the oncologist.
"I'm her boyfriend" he says, with his 'don't mess with me mate' voice.
The consult began. He told me that the results are not what they would have hoped for. The treatment I have had was making me worse. I was given a choice and asked whether I would like to stay here in the hospital, or if I would like to go to a hospice where a place was booked for me, or if I would like to go home.

Easy, "I'll go home," I was delighted. In my mind at that point I'd thought it was good news as people go home from hospital when they were well enough to do so.
"No more hospital."

I certainly was not going to go to a hospice as people who go there, I had thought, go there to die.

The consultant explained that these options were given because I might be better cared for at a hospice or at home.
He asked if I had any questions.
So I asked, "Is this cancer then?"
"Yes."
Finally, I had an admission, a diagnosis.
Mum said, "Is that it then?"
"Well" he said, "you have those funny little pills" pointing to the homeopathic medicine and then, pointing to the ceiling, he said "and Him up there", I think he meant God. He told me to "have a good Christmas" and gave my final prescription and left my bedside.

Unknown to me then, Judith went after the consultant and explained that the family needed to know and needed to prepare itself. How long does she have?
She was told maybe 3 months.
The nurse rang the hospital pharmacy to order my drugs to go home with. We waited and we waited some more. It was coming up to an hour and still no drugs.

"Forget it" Mum says "let's go".

We told no one. My possessions were gathered. I was hurtled down the hospital corridors in my wheelchair. What was the point of waiting for drugs when I'd been told their treatment was making me worse?

I clambered into the car. "Have you taken back my wheelchair to the ward mum?"

"Leave it by the door, let's just go."

"Way da go Mum," I thought.

A defiant act, a symbolic two fingered flick to them.

Chapter 6 - Lemon Drizzle Cake

I was at my parent's house and was continuing with the homoeopathy. I'd been there for at least 9 or 10 months and Allan had been there with me all that time, having taken unpaid leave from his job. Seeing that I had recovered rather dramatically, he had returned to London and to his job, feeling confident I wasn't about to drop dead now. It was around that time when I really felt that I was going to get better.

Janice had advised me in one our consultation to do something creative. I asked her , "Could I make a cake and decorate it beautifully as that would be really creative." However, I remembered that Janice had put me on a very strict eating regime which meant that I could not to eat anything with sugar in it or any refined food, so that meant no white flour either.

"What's the point of making a cake if you can't eat it?" I questioned her as my beautiful, creative cake I had in mind did not include brown flour and or the exclusion of sugar.
"You always want your cake and eat it," Janice retorted.
"You could always make cakes for other people," she suggested.
"That would be self-inflicted torture, Janice."

After some banter, we finally sorted out that if I made a cake, I could have a very thin slice of it.

I was overjoyed, sugar, cake, YUMMY food again!!
"So if I make, let's say 20 cakes, can I have a small, thin, slice of all of them?" I queried.
"I suppose so."
I thought this was going to be simply amazing and I was ready to bounce back to Mum's kitchen. In reality, I plodded slowly and carefully down Janice's stairs to my Dad's awaiting car.
All I could think of was the cake I was about to bake. It would be the most delicious one ever, with all the most delicious ingredients because I could eat a slice of it. Thick, sticky, dark chocolate cake. I couldn't wait to set to it. Mum – a great cook - had most of the ingredients in her kitchen already, but not all of them.

So I matched the recipes up with the ingredients available at the time. I would have had to wait another day to make a chocolate cake, so, Lemon Drizzle cake it was.

Gas Mark 4 / 180°C
35 minutes

8" Cake tin with loose bottom, lined and greased with collar

Beat together:

6oz self-raising flour

1 level tsp baking powder

2 eggs

4oz soft margarine

6oz castor sugar

Rind 1 lemon

6 tbsp milk

Cook and leave in tin

Skewer cake

Spread on topping

Leave until cold

Topping - 6oz castor sugar

Juice of lemon

I was so looking forward to eating it. I hadn't had sugar for what seemed like ages. I'd missed it terribly. However, first, I was to wait until it had cooled before spearing it several times with a skewer and pouring the lemon topping on. Then I had to wait for the topping to set.

It tasted like manna from heaven. It melted in my mouth and was by far the most wonderful food I had ever tasted. My lips smacked loudly and my taste buds sang, MMMM. It was the best and most memorable slice of cake I'd ever had.

Chapter 7 - Something Worth Considering

A friend of mine, who had kindly agreed to proof read my first manuscript attempt said, "They will want to see that you have done something amazing with your life."

I put this to my sister and she said, "What do you mean? You already have, haven't you?"

"Yeah, I think so." I grin.

"Surviving terminal brain cancer is pretty damn good. Not only that but surviving terminal brain cancer with the aid of alternative therapy."

At the time that I am writing this, cancer statistics from cancer research say 1 in 2 people born after 1960 in the UK will be diagnosed with some form of cancer in their life time. Read more at http://www.cancerresearchuk.org/health-professional/cancer-statistics/risk/lifetime-risk#iSl2F3LYjlOSCBKZ.99

The UK has one of the worst statistics for cancer. We must be doing something wrong.

My learning and thoughts on the current medical procedures for cancer patients of cutting out parts of the body, burning and or poisoning it without any other therapy, is barbaric and is just binding your time. It might give you a little longer but I don't feel it is going to getting to the cause of the cancer. If this is what you want to do then of course that is fine. We all have our own choices of what we hope will guide us to health. For me, I know I wouldn't do any of that again. I want to make sure I would continue with my life fully, not simply prolong it whilst at the same time live with cancer.

I would definitely want to make sure I did as much as I can not to get cancer again. I am not the only one to think this way, it seems. There are a number of studies and reports that suggest that some doctors would actually choose alternatives for themselves and their families. The report, conducted by Stanford University in 2014, suggests that: 'Most American doctors would decline aggressive treatment if they were dying. Researchers looked at the responses of nearly 1,100 doctors in California who took part in a 2013 survey about their end-of-life care preferences and 790 doctors in Arkansas, who completed a similar survey in 1989.' (https://consumer.healthday.com/senior-citizen-information-31/misc-aging-news-10/facing-death-most-u-s-doctors-would-decline-extraordinary-measures-688172.html retrieved on 28th July 2016.)

As I am writing this, I tried to find this information on The Stanford University website but it no longer presents that information; I wonder where it went? The same research was also cited in a Daily Mail article.
(http://www.dailymail.co.uk/health/article-2643751/Most-doctors-terminally-ill-AVOID-aggressive-treatments-chemotherapy-despite-recommending-patients.html retrieved on 29th July 2016.)

Most doctors who were terminally ill would AVOID aggressive treatments such as chemotherapy - despite recommending it to their patients. It also states that 88% of doctors would choose 'do not resuscitate' orders for themselves. At the same time, it also suggests that most pursue aggressive, life-prolonging treatments for patients. Could this be because the medical system rewards doctors for taking action or because a leap into the apparent unknown world of alternative remedy is too risky for them professionally? The researchers say there is a 'tipping point' where the high-intensity treatment becomes more of a burden than the disease itself.

The way I see it, from what I have learned from homoeopathy, a tumour, the lump, the itchy mole, the constant cough, in fact any symptom is a sign that something isn't quite right in the body. Cells may change from normal cells to toxic cells for various reasons. This will NOT apply to everybody as we all have different levels of immunity and tolerance. For example you wake up in the morning and may be affected by the electric pylon you've been living by for years. Eat a high sugar breakfast with E numbers and then leave the house with your mobile phone on in the pocket just by your heart and then talk on your mobile phone for a long time holding it just by your brain. Just walking down your road you may inhale too much petrol from the exhaust fumes, be affected by masts, and so it goes on throughout the day.

Sally Ann Hutcheson, a naturopath, explains that "Toxins are many and various. Trouble is caused not by one toxin, but by an aggregate of toxins built up over the years coupled with deficiencies" A broad category of toxins are:

> **Chemical (External)** toxins such as insecticides, household cleaners, cosmetics, antiperspirants, soap, toothpaste, food

additives, drugs, vaccines, chemicals in water and air pollutants.

Chemical (Internal) made by the body such as excess adrenalin, hormones, dead cells.

Hereditary/Genetic such as emotional stress, worry, anxiety, grief, anger, insult and so on.

Also **perverse energy** - electro-magnetic, electricity, geopathic, radiation (from mobile phones, aero planes, power lines and cables, x-rays, computers, TVs, for example).

Deficiency of: nutrients, exercise, sunlight, water rest and love.

The cancer is part of you and not an alien thing. I heard a great analogy for this from Edward Evans talk on **www.thetruthaboutcancer.com.** If you see a flashing light on the dashboard in your car, you need to fix something in the engine and not just get a new battery for the flashing light. This will just cover up the symptom.

If you feel that your health is going downhill and want to get better you need to take a leap and make some changes in your life and circumstances. It's not rocket science.

You may have seen the film *Ground Hog Day.* If you keep doing the same thing you will get the same result If it is not working for you then do something different and you'll get a different outcome. It could be anything from stopping working in an environment where you are inhaling toxic fumes or getting some therapy to help you deal with for example, the bully in the playground, office or house.

You probably can't get other people to change their actions but you can change yourself. There is great example of this on the CD www.thesecret.tv where their vision is to bring joy to billions. Take at the look.

Forgive that person who said those hurtful words, that violent assault, be it mental, emotional or physical. It may still be hurting you but I'd bet that the perpetrator hasn't given it a thought.

In my clinic, I have found that many of my clients hold on to old thoughts and events that maybe date from years ago, even childhood, and these still affect them. There will be several ways to disperse these feelings of anger, hate, bitterness and so on. Of course I am championing homoeopathy, but as a first step here is a practical and therapeutic procedure, which may also be helpful. Get some paper and a pen and write out all these feelings. Put in all these swear words and the words you'd wished you'd had said to the bully, the abuser, the adulterer. Write out a few A4 sides of paper of this, not just a couple of sentences. When you're done, go outside, get a metal bin and burn all of it. The results of this can be powerfully cathartic and aid in the healing process.

I could go on forever and explain more about other therapies: Narayani remedies, Flower Essences, New Vistas combinations, suggest books, cancer diets, urge you to look at the episodes on The Truth about Cancer, exercise, consider life changes such as reducing long working hours, meditation, look at relationships, living environment and other complementary therapies. This not a text book. I'm leaving it up to you to do the research.

In doing this it will mean that YOU really want to get better. It's YOU that needs to seek out what's best for you. This book is a story about my experiences and hopes to inspire others to investigate other options to find better health.

I wish you all good health and happiness.
Gemma

Chapter 8 - Medical Notes

DEPARTMENT OF NEUROSURGERY:

Direct Line: 0171-346 3284
Fax No: 0171-346 3280

BC/KJH

9th February 1996

Dr ▓▓▓
Barton House,
233, Albion Road,
London N16 9JT

Dear Dr ▓▓▓

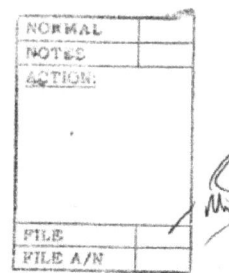

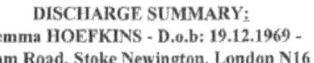

King's Healthcare NHS Trust
King's College Hospital
Denmark Hill, London, SE5 9RS
Telephone: 0171-737 4000
Facsimile: 0171-346 3445
Direct telephone line

DISCHARGE SUMMARY:
Gemma HOEFKINS - D.o.b: 19.12.1969 -
9, Chesham Road, Stoke Newington, London N16 0DP:

Hospital No: Z001504
Admission Date: 29.01.1996
Discharge Date: 03.02.1996
Diagnosis: Pineal Tumour - Previous Ventricular Peritoneal Shunt
Operation: Stereotactic Biopsy

This 26 year old lady was admitted for an MR guided stereotactic biopsy of her pineal lesion. At the age of 22 she was diagnosed as having hydrocephalus of unknown etiology. A VP shunt was inserted at St. Bartholomew's Hospital. In 1994 she underwent an MR scan of the brain, this showed a lesion in the mid brain region causing acqueductal stenosis. She was serially MR scanned and this initially showed no tumour progression, she was therefore treated conservatively. However she found the uncertainty a constant worry, and felt restricted in her activities being a young woman of 26. She underwent a further gadolinium enhanced MR scan on 20th December 1995. This showed enhancement of the hypothalamic and peri-aqueductal lesion, and a further enhancing lesion was seen in the IV ventricle. The appearances were thought to be consistent with a tumour arising in the region of the pineal and spreading through the CSF, likely to be a dysgerminoma. Tumour markers both in blood and CSF so far have been negative. Her only symptoms at the moment are occasional dizziness and intermittent double vision when looking to the left. There was no Parinaud's sign and her gait was normal. Clinical examination was otherwise unremarkable.

Operation:

She underwent a MR guided stereotactic biopsy through a right parietal burr hole on 1st February 1996.

C/Forward.....

B/Forward.....Gemma HOEFKINS

Post Operatively:

She made a prompt recovery.

Histology:

The initial smear result suggested that this was a low grade pineocytoma, however further electron microscopy is due to be performed before the final histology report is issued.

She was discharged home without any medication on 3rd February 1996. She will be seen in the next available out-patient clinic.

Yours sincerely,

Mr.
Registrar to Mr   FRCS MRCP
Consultant Neurosurgeon.

c.c.   Dr. Ray Chaudhuri, Consultant Neurologist, King's College Hospital.

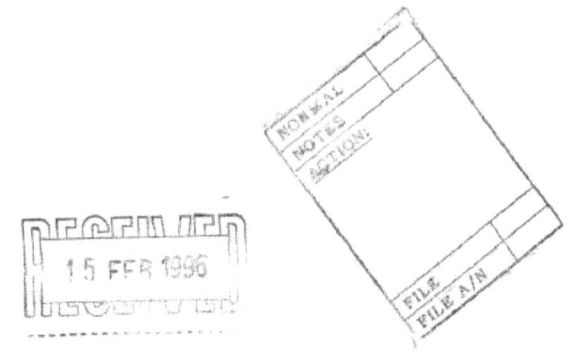

**THE ROYAL
HOSPITALS
NHS TRUST**

RADIOTHERAPY/CLINICAL ONCOLOGY

ST BARTHOLOMEW'S HOSPITAL
WEST SMITHFIELD
LONDON EC1A 7BE

RECEPTION 071 601 8357/8
FAX 071 601 8364

Mr ▓▓▓
Consultant Neurosurgeon
King's College Hospital
Denmark Hill
London SE5 9RS

PNP/EJV/F786854

11 March 1996

Dear ▓▓▓

Gemma HOEFKINS DOB 19/12/69
9 Chesholm Road Stoke Newington London N16 0DP

Subsequent to my letter's dated the 21 February and 4 March, I regret to inform you that after re-viewing the films with our neuroradiologist, we have seen a separate focus of tumour caudal to the primary in the aqueduct and another in the suprasellar region. I am going to MRI the entire neuraxis and may need to alter the treatment plan. I will keep you informed.

Yours sincerely

Consultant Radiotherapist

cc Dr ▓▓▓
    Barton House
    233 Albion Road

BC/MC/Z001504
Mr ▓▓▓▓▓▓ 6.3.96

19 March 1996

KING'S COLLEGE HOSPITAL (DENMARK HILL)
Denmark Hill, London SE5 9RS
Tel: 0171-737 4000 Fax: 0171 346 3445

Dr ▓▓▓
Barton House
233 Albion Road
London
N16 9JT

Dear Dr ▓▓▓

Gemma Hoefkens d.o.b. 19.12.69
9 Chesham Road, Stoke Newington, London N16 ODP

I reviewed Gemma Hoefkens. As you know, she was recently an in-patient and underwent a stereotactic biopsy of her pineal tumour, which has turned out to be a pineocytoma. She has already been seen by the Radiotherapist, Dr ▓▓▓▓ and had her mask made today, with a view to starting radiotherapy next week. She has some persistent diplopia on looking down and to the left and there was one dizzy episode recently, after washing her hair. Otherwise, she remains extremely well.

Her acuities are 6/4 bilaterally and her fundi were essentially normal. There was no visual inattention. I have organised a lateral skull X-ray today to check the setting of her Medos valve. We will be seeing her next after completion of radiotherapy.

Yours sincerely

Mr ▓▓▓▓▓▓▓▓s
Registrar to Mr ▓▓▓▓▓▓ FRCS MRCP
Consultant Neurosurgeon

THE ROYAL HOSPITALS NHS TRUST

RADIOTHERAPY/CLINICAL ONCOLOGY

ST BARTHOLOMEW'S HOSPITAL
WEST SMITHFIELD
LONDON EC1A 7BE

RECEPTION: 071 601 8357/8
FAX: 071 601 8364

Mr
Consultant Neurosurgeon
King's College Hospital
Denmark Hill
London SE5 9RS

PNP/EJV/F786854

5 June 1996

Dear

Gemma HOEFKENS DOB 19/12/69
9 Chesholm Road London N16 0DP

Subsequent to my several letters to you concerning this young lady, she is now about to complete her course of radiotherapy. You will remember that our preoperative staging showed that her pineal mass was extending through the aduaduct region and that there was a second intracranial mass in the pituitary region. You will also recall that the spinal MRI scan showed numerous small punctate areas of high signal lining the cord which was scattered throughout the whole of the spine suggesting spinal metastases. I therefore undertook craniospinal radiotherapy and by our usual 6 mv x-ray technique, delivered a dose of 3500 cGy in 21 fractions over 42 days to the whole neuraxis. In the second phase of treatment, the pineal midbrain and anterior third ventricular region (encompassing the second intracranial mass) received an additional 1500 cGy in 9 fractions. Gemma felt very tired towards the end of treatment and needed to be admitted to hospital.

I plan to repeat her MRI scan and will write again with the findings.

Yours sincerely

P N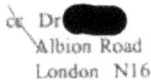
Consultant Radiotherapist

cc Dr
    Albion Road
    London N16

THE ROYAL HOSPITAL OF ST BARTHOLOMEW, THE ROYAL LONDON HOSPITAL AND THE LONDON CHEST HOSPITAL NHS TRUST

RADIOTHERAPY/CLINICAL ONCOLOGY

ST BARTHOLOMEW'S HOSPITAL
WEST SMITHFIELD
LONDON EC1A 7BE

RECEPTION: 071 601 8357/8
FAX: 071 601 8364

THE ROYAL
HOSPITALS
NHS TRUST

Our ref: SE/EJV/F786854

20 June 1996

Dr
Barton House
233 Albion Road
London N16 9JT

Dear Dr

Gemma HOEFKINS DOB 19/12/69
9 Chesham Road Stoke Newington London N16 0DP

Diagnosis: Pineocytoma with spinal drop metastases

This 26 year old lady with worsening memory and diplopia since 1994, was diagnosed with a pineocytoma in February of this year. An MRI scan reviewed by the neuroradiologists at St Bartholomews showed a mass in the aqueduct/fourth ventricular region and a further focus of tumour chordal to this area and a separate focus in the suprasellar region. In addition am MRI of her neuraxis revealed the presence of spinal drop metastases.

She was commenced on craniospinal radiotherapy on the 22 April and completed her radiotherapy on the 7 June. She received 3500 cGy in 21 fractions to the whole cranium and spine, followed by a further 1500 cGy in 9 fractions to the midbrain. During the second phase of her radiotherapy, she was admitted to Heath Harrison Ward with nausea and vomiting and increased dizziness. This was associated with headaches. Clinically there were no focal neurological signs apart from ataxia of gait. A CT scan of her head showed the previous primary tumour but there was no evidence of raised intracranial pressure. She symptomatically improved on oral Dexamethasone and at the completion of her radiotherapy, was mobile independently with no obvious ataxia. She is still experiencing some vertigo but this has significantly improved.

THE ROYAL HOSPITAL OF ST BARTHOLOMEW, THE ROYAL LONDON HOSPITAL AND THE LONDON CHEST HOSPITAL NHS TRUST

TRUST OFFICE	DR S J ARNOTT	-	(TEL 071 601 8353)	DR G MAIR
THE ROYAL LONDON HOSPITAL	DR A J MUNRO	-	(TEL 071 601 8355)	DR B MANTELL
WHITECHAPEL	DR F N FLOWMAN	-	(TEL 071 601 8351)	DR P NEAVE
LONDON E1 1BB				

RADIOTHERAPY/CLINICAL ONCOLOGY

ST BARTHOLOMEW'S HOSPITAL
WEST SMITHFIELD
LONDON EC1A 7BE

RECEPTION: 071 601 8357/8
FAX: 071 601 8364

THE ROYAL
HOSPITALS
NHS TRUST

Our ref: SH/EJV/F/86854   23 July 1996

Dr
Barton House
233 Albion Road
London N16 9JT

Dear Dr

Gemma HOEFKINS DOB 19/12/69
9 Chesholm Road Stoke Newington London N16 0DP

This patient with pineocytoma with 2 intracranial foci and drop metastases in the spine returned to clinic today a month after completing craniospinal radiotherapy. Although she has gradually improving her herself, she remains unsteady, which has worsened by reducing her Dexamethasone beyond 6 mgs daily and she has developed double vision in all directions except for left lateral gaze in the past week. She has had no headaches or vomiting.

On examination today the patient looks well. Her fundi was normal and there are no focal neurological deficits detectable.

A recent CT scan shows that there is still enhancing tissue extending from the region of the pineal through the aquaduct to the fourth ventricle and the optic chiasm although it is less extensive than in March. The drop metastases within the spine have disappeared.

I have discussed the patient with Dr who has suggested that we proceed to a PET scan to see whether this is active tumour. Gemma understands that she may need to proceed to chemotherapy following this and we will see her again in a fortnight to discuss treatment with her. In the meantime I have left her on Dexamethasone 6 mgs daily.

Yours sincerely

Dr
Senior Registrar to

THE ROYAL HOSPITALS OF ST BARTHOLOMEW, THE ROYAL LONDON HOSPITAL AND THE LONDON CHEST HOSPITAL NHS TRUST

TRUST OFFICE	DR S J ARNOTT	-	(TEL 071 601 8355)	DR G MAIR
THE ROYAL LONDON HOSPITAL	DR A J MUNRO	-	(TEL 071 601 8355)	DR B MANTELL
WHITECHAPEL	DR P N PLOWMAN	-	(TEL 071 601 8355)	DR F NEAVE
LONDON E1 1BB				

RADIOTHERAPY/CLINICAL ONCOLOGY

ST BARTHOLOMEW'S HOSPITAL
WEST SMITHFIELD
LONDON EC1A 7BE

RECEPTION: 071 601 8357/8
FAX: 071 601 8364

THE ROYAL
HOSPITALS
NHS TRUST

Our ref: PNP/EJV/F786854

6 August 1996

Mr P█████
Consultant Neurosurgeon
King's College Hospital
Denmark Hill
London SE5 9RS

Dear █████

Gemma HOEFKINS DOB 19.12.69
9 Chesholm Road London N16 0DP

Subsequent to our recent correspondance, this young lady's repeat MRI scan of the neuraxis shows that the cranial lesions are smaller and that the spinal metastases have disappeared following spinal radiotherapy. However, Gemma has developed diplopia on central gaze, finds it difficult to come off steroids and there does remain enhancing mass tissue - particularly from the pineal area and extending down around the aqueduct. Furthermore a PET scan which I performed last week shows that the tumour is viable in this area.

I am sure that we ought to finish her treatment course by the same chemotherapy that we give for pineoblastoma (as this pineocytoma has certainly "declared itself" as an aggressive metastasising tumour of that lineage). I have discussed this with the patient and her mother today and we are getting her in for her first course. Following 3 courses I will repeat the scan and write again.

Yours sincerely

P N█████
Consultant Radiotherapist

cc Dr █████, Barton House, 233 Albion Road, London N16 9JT

THE ROYAL HOSPITAL OF ST BARTHOLOMEW, THE ROYAL LONDON HOSPITAL AND THE LONDON CHEST HOSPITAL NHS TRUST

TRUST OFFICE	DR S J ARNOTT	(TEL 071 601 8353)	DR O MAIR
THE ROYAL LONDON HOSPITAL	DR A J MUNRO	(TEL 071 601 8353)	DR B MANTELL
WHITECHAPEL	DR P N PLOWMAN	(TEL 071 601 8351)	DR F NEAVE
LONDON E1 1BB			

THE ROYAL
HOSPITALS
NHS TRUST

ST BARTHOLOMEW'S HOSPITAL
WEST SMITHFIELD
LONDON EC1A 7BE

RECEPTION: 071 601 8357/8
FAX: 071 601 8364

Our ref: AF/EJV/F786854

19 November 1996

Dr ▮
Barton House
233 Albion Road
London N16 9JT

Dear Dr ▮

RE: Gemma HOEFKENS   DOB 19/12/69
9 Chesholm Road London N16 0DP

Gemma was admitted to Heath Harrison Ward on the 13 November for reassessment of her overall condition. As outlined in previous letters, she presented with aqueduct stenosis in 1992. By 1994 a peri-aqueductal mass was apparent and was found to be a pineocytoma, subsequently with spinal metastases. Craniospinal radiotherapy was given with initial good result but her symptoms worsened again and 3 cycles of VEJ chemotherapy were given. Her condition deteriorated markedly after the first cycle and an MRI scan was done which showed reduction in the tumour size. However Gemma's condition continued to deteriorate. Prior at this admission she had had ptosis for 2 weeks such that she had to hold her eye open. She had also been increasingly drowsy with headache and weakness in the limbs. She was taking Dexamethasone 10 mgs daily, Co-Danthrusate 1 tablet bd, Prochlorperazine 5 mgs daily and Omeprazole 20 mgs daily. She has been living with her parents at Worcestershire because she was unable to manage at her own flat in Stoke Newington. MRI scanning undertaken the day before her admission showed marked progression of the primary, with new deposits in the anterior parts of the lateral ventricles and suprasellar area. Imaging of the spine was not undertaken and there are no plans to do so.

Research on Homoeopathy:

http://s-scrutton.co.uk/DIEs/illness-a-c/cancer.html

http://hpathy.com/scientific-research/research-in-homoeopathy/

http://hpathy.com/scientific-research/research-in-homeopathy-3/

http://drnancymalik.wordpress.com/article/scientific-research-in-homeopathy/

http://www.ncbi.nlm.nih.gov/pubmed/23652641

http://www.homeoinst.org/document-archive

http://www.nationalcenterforhomeopathy.org/content/indisputable-evidence-for-homeopathic-remedies

http://drnancymalik.wordpress.com/article/scientific-research-in-homeopathy/

http://avilian.co.uk/2008/08/scientific-research-and-homeopathy-plant-studi es/

http://www.homeoinst.org/sites/default/files/uploads/u-3/HRI_ResearchArticle_18_Winter2012_Harrison_HELAT.pdf
http://www.ncbi.nlm.nih.gov/pubmed/16815514
http://www.ncbi.nlm.nih.gov/pmc/articles/PMC2958565
http://www.ncbi.nlm.nih.gov/pubmed/15532695

http://www.ncbi.nlm.nih.gov/pubmed/11479779

http://www.ncbi.nlm.nih.gov/pubmed/15532696
http://www.ncbi.nlm.nih.gov/pubmed/17101037
http://www.ncbi.nlm.nih.gov/pubmed/18826582
http://www.ncbi.nlm.nih.gov/pubmed/16296916
http://www.ncbi.nlm.nih.gov/pubmed/17004404

http://www.ncbi.nlm.nih.gov/pubmed/17544864

www.homeopathic.com

http://homeopathyplus.com.au/chronicillness.pdf

http://www.blueskyin.com/people-die-from-chemotherapy-not-cancer-said-doctor-peter-glidden

GEMMA WOULD LIKE TO THANK......

Mum and dad, my sisters and brothers, Allan, Anna, Sue for all your love and support. Janice for being my amazing homoeopath (just a note Janice passed away in 2005 and is missed by many and her legacy of her work as a homoeopath remains), Sally Ann, Nicky for continuing her good work. My friends and family for all those visits to my bedside, Annie for her encouragement with my book, Collette for deciphering my medical notes, Steve for advising me with my befuddled initial chapters, Victoria and Geraldine, my longest friend – in time not height, for her help with my book and computer and last but not least, my lovely, caring, understanding current partner. Allan and I didn't make it and broke up but strangely enough my new man is also called Allan, who helped me with the social media to get this book out there.

Lightning Source UK Ltd.
Milton Keynes UK
UKHW022008070422
401245UK00009B/2222